T0017026

Evangelicalism: A Very Short Introduction

VERY SHORT INTRODUCTIONS are for anyone wanting a stimulating and accessible way into a new subject. They are written by experts, and have been translated into more than 45 different languages.

The series began in 1995, and now covers a wide variety of topics in every discipline. The VSI library currently contains over 700 volumes—a Very Short Introduction to everything from Psychology and Philosophy of Science to American History and Relativity—and continues to grow in every subject area.

Very Short Introductions available now:

Available soon:

For more information visit our website

www.oup.com/vsi/

John G. Stackhouse Jr.

EVANGELICALISM

A Very Short Introduction

OXFORD
UNIVERSITY PRESS

OXFORD

UNIVERSITY PRESS

Oxford University Press is a department of the University of Oxford.
It furthers the University's objective of excellence in research, scholarship,
and education by publishing worldwide. Oxford is a registered trade mark of
Oxford University Press in the UK and certain other countries.

Published in the United States of America by Oxford University Press
198 Madison Avenue, New York, NY 10016, United States of America.

© Oxford University Press 2022

Library of Congress Cataloging-in-Publication Data

Names: Stackhouse, John G. (John Gordon), 1960– author.
Title: Evangelicalism : a very short introduction / John G. Stackhouse Jr.
Description: New York, NY : Oxford University Press, [2022] |
Series: Very short introduction | Includes bibliographical references and index.
Identifiers: LCCN 2021061977 (print) | LCCN 2021061978 (ebook) |
ISBN 9780190079680 (paperback) | ISBN 9780190079703 (epub) |
ISBN 9780190079697 (ebook)
Subjects: LCSH: Evangelicalism.
Classification: LCC BR1640 .S6835 2022 (print) | LCC BR1640 (ebook) |
DDC 289.9/5—dc23/eng/20220204
LC record available at https://lccn.loc.gov/2021061977
LC ebook record available at https://lccn.loc.gov/2021061978

1 3 5 7 9 8 6 4 2

Printed in Great Britain by
Ashford Colour Press Ltd., Gosport, Hants., on acid-free paper

To George
evangelical interpreter *ne plus ultra*

Contents

List of illustrations

Acknowledgments

I wrote this book as an evangelical, a faithful and critical member of a family that, especially in the institutions of the InterVarsity Christian Fellowship, Wheaton College, *Christianity Today* magazine, and Regent College, has both blessed and wounded me. For reasons that will not interest the reader, this book had to be written under unusual constraints. I therefore had to rely on the kindness of a few friendly colleagues in the revision of the manuscript when I would have much preferred to draw for advice on a much wider array of regional specialists. If one simply must settle for a mere trio of helpers in such a task, however, one could not do better than the globally informed Mark Hutchinson, Mark Noll, and Brian Stanley. I thank them here once more for their timely and percipient assistance in both correcting and augmenting my work in numerous ways.

My longtime Oxford editor, Cynthia Read, kindly introduced me to my new Oxford editor, Nancy Toff, and I am once again glad to be working under the gentle but firm strictures of this excellent house. Nancy's sharp eye and educated ear made this book look and sound much better than it did. Thanks also to Zara Cannon-Mohammed at OUP for cheerful and capable help with the illustrations. I gratefully acknowledge the Stephen and Ella Steeves Endowment at Crandall University for research support and the researchers thus supported: the estimable Maria Hovey,

Dani Reimer, and Kira Smith. Maria also skillfully prepared the index.

I am grateful for the supportive company of Kari and Devon Stackhouse in North Vancouver and colleague Keith Bodner in Moncton over the course of this project, as well as for the prayers of Trevor, Zenith, and Jude Stackhouse Bose and Joshua Stackhouse and Lauren Morgan—some of my very favorite evangelicals. I humbly acknowledge Mark Noll and Martin Marty as the two mentors who have best modeled to me concision and clarity in sketching complex matters of religious history. And I dedicate this volume to George Marsden, who has inspired and encouraged me, as he has so many others, for forty years.

Feast of the Transfiguration, 2021
Moncton, New Brunswick

Introduction

Imagine an evangelical.

He is white, middle-aged, and middle-class. He pastors a large Baptist church in the American Midwest or Sunbelt. He also holds large meetings in various other cities, which combine a rally of the faithful with an invitation to newcomers to convert. He probably has his own radio or television show, or at least a popular podcast. He preaches frequently on current social controversies, and he aligns himself conspicuously with the political Right.

This, we should say more carefully, is a *stereotypical* evangelical, at least in the minds of many. The truly *typical* evangelical in the world of the early twenty-first century looks very different.

The typical evangelical of the 2020s is not a "he." *She* is also not white, and she is probably a shopkeeper, clerk, or artisan living somewhere in sub-Saharan Africa or in a Latin American city. She has no public voice, but she sings in her church's choir, teaches the Sunday school class of one of her children, and leads a literacy workshop for poor women in her neighborhood. She rarely discusses social or political issues, but she beams when she relates how her husband's conversion ended his alcohol abuse on wild weekends. This is your statistically typical evangelical Christian.

However, not only the news media, but also the historical accounts of evangelicalism are dominated by white, middle-class, English-speaking male preachers. Who are (all) the evangelicals, then, really? Answering that question is the chief goal of this book.

Evangelicalism in the twenty-first century is global, growing on every continent—except where it began. While evangelicals slowly fade from the scene in Europe, America, and "Greater" Britain (the United Kingdom, Canada, Australia, and New Zealand), evangelicals are thriving across Africa, throughout Latin America, in South Korea, in China—even in Indonesia and Iran.

Moreover, evangelicals increasingly wield cultural influence well beyond church life. Evangelicals lead and support major nongovernmental organizations that provide a dazzling array of services to developing countries around the world. They continue to found and run schools: from day-care centers to trade schools to universities, not just Bible colleges and seminaries. In many countries they now form significant voting constituencies capable of influencing municipal, regional, and even national elections. And they even influence popular culture, whether by showing up in mainstream movies and music (from Denzel Washington to Justin Bieber) or by maintaining their own large parallel industry of made-for-evangelical movies and so-called Christian contemporary music, industries that now generate hundreds of millions of dollars.

So who are the evangelicals? Where do they come from? What do they want? What are they up to? And, not incidentally, how can the same people produce an American president such as Jimmy Carter and support an American president such as Donald Trump?

This Very Short Introduction is not simply, or even primarily, an abbreviated history of evangelicalism, although it does trace a generally diachronic arc. Its main purpose is to acquaint the

1. **Bishop Haywood preaches at Bread of Life Church in Wisconsin, USA. African-American evangelicals often defy white stereotypes regarding gender roles, especially in church.**

reader with the character of evangelicalism, with its peculiar nature. The parallel is absurdly grandiose, but just as the Gospels themselves set out the general progress of Jesus's life while fairly freely grouping material to make thematic points, the career of evangelicalism demonstrates the original and abiding central qualities of evangelicalism as the theme of this volume.

Evangelicalism traces its roots back to the Bible itself—which is fitting enough, since evangelicals describe themselves as Bible people. But evangelicalism as a definite something arises out of the Protestant Reformation of the sixteenth century and then takes shape via the English movement of Puritanism and the middle European movement of Pietism in the seventeenth century. It blossoms into the transatlantic revivals of the eighteenth century, the era of the movement's ancestors, such as itinerant preacher George Whitefield, pastor and theologian Jonathan Edwards, and the brothers John and Charles Wesley, the former evangelicalism's premier organizer and the latter its leading hymnwriter. From this era of the "ur-evangelicals" the story goes global, such that today evangelicalism is one of the largest and most lively social movements on the planet, touching almost every culture and deeply influencing hundreds of millions of people from Johannesburg to Jakarta.

But what sort of thing *is* evangelicalism? A checklist of doctrines? A set of convictions? A coordinated ecclesiastical movement? A recurring impulse to renewal? A particular style of religion? We will arrive at a qualified "yes" to all of these alternatives, and more, because evangelicals are perhaps best understood as simply vital, mainstream Protestant Christians, committed to the gospel (the "evangel"), its proclamation, and its implications for all of life— and doing whatever they can to further the gospel's reach.

Chapter 1
Original evangelicalism

Back to the Bible. Evangelicals reflexively define themselves in terms of the Bible, and histories of evangelicalism often have traced it back to the sacred scriptures of Christianity. *Evangelical*, after all, stems from *evangel* (Greek: *euaggelion*), the word translated "good news" in modern Bible versions and "gospel" in older ones. Evangelicals see themselves as focused on, redeemed by, and commissioned to proclaim the good news of God's salvation through Jesus Christ. The Bible is the divinely inspired account of that salvation. So evangelicals are "Bible people." The great evangelical leader John Wesley, arguably one of the best-read people of his erudite age, and himself the issuer of over 400 publications as author, editor, or publisher, called himself *homo unius libri*, a man of one book.

Every Christian, however, would claim to revere the Bible as God's written Word. Roman Catholic, Orthodox, Protestant: all Christians are Bible people. And all of them view their churches as stemming from the career of Jesus. What else could they think?

Evangelicals differ from Catholics and Orthodox Christians in that they champion the Bible as the supremely authoritative guide to faith and life. Their Catholic and Orthodox siblings hold to the idea that the Holy Spirit of God continued to teach the Christian church new things over the centuries since the composition of the

New Testament in the first century. The church was led by that same Spirit to receive these teachings as divinely given and thus came to respect tradition alongside the Bible as a religious authority as well—not unlike the way Jews regard the Talmud and Muslims regard the Hadith. And, like Jews and Muslims, Catholics and Orthodox differ among themselves about just how authoritative that tradition should be understood to be.

Evangelicals, by contrast, have tended to be suspicious of what grew up in the centuries after the apostolic age. As Martin Luther memorably put it in his appearance before the 1521 Diet of Worms, an imperial hearing to ascertain his orthodoxy, "Unless I am convinced of error by the testimony of Scripture or (since I put no trust in the unsupported authority of Pope or councils, since it is plain that they have often erred and often contradicted themselves) by clear reasoning, I stand convinced by the Scriptures to which I have appealed. My conscience is subject to God's Word." Evangelicals see themselves not just as generic Christians who accept the Bible as inspired, but also as Protestant Christians who give singular authority to the Bible and cast a gimlet eye on any other claims on the Christian conscience.

Indeed, the self-understanding of evangelicals tends to leap directly from the pages of the Bible to the Reformation of the sixteenth century. A few determined historians of evangelicalism attempted to trace a sacred thread of biblical faithfulness through what they regarded as dark ages, with perhaps an approving nod toward the great early theologian Augustine along the way. Such an errand into the historiographical wilderness, alas, has often resulted in the evangelical family tree including such medieval Gnostic groups as the Paulicians, Bogomils, and Cathars. In the spirit of "the enemy of my enemy is my friend," these movements possessed the vital redeeming quality in the eyes of evangelical chroniclers that they were persecuted by Rome. But their wildly deviant doctrines disqualify them as protoevangelicals.

The lineage of evangelicalism becomes both more plausible and more clear when the narrative turns to the Waldensians, a thirteenth-century spiritual movement of uncompromising rigor that arose in Lyon, France. Persecution by the Roman Catholic authorities drove them into the French and Italian Alps, where a remnant eventually influenced the important Swiss Protestant reformer Heinrich Bullinger in the later sixteenth century. The Protestant movement eventually claimed them as forerunners, and their descendants mostly merged with sixteenth- and seventeenth-century Protestant communities. (There remain distinct Waldensian churches in those regions and in the Italian diaspora.)

Even more clearly setting the stage for Luther and company were John Wycliffe and the English Lollard movement of the late fourteenth and fifteenth centuries, as well as Wycliffe's younger contemporary, Jan Hus, and his fellow Bohemian reformers. These were all "Bible movements" that called to account various late medieval excesses or deficiencies in the name of scripture—such as the widespread traffic in amulets, images, relics, and pilgrimages, which smacked of mere magic, on the one hand, and ignorant priests and negligent bishops who failed to educate or even regularly preach to their congregations on the other. They therefore championed the translation of the Bible into the vernacular and the reading of the Bible beyond the cadre of priests. And each of these movements was deemed too radical—in the strict sense of *radix*, going back to "the root" of Christianity in scripture at the expense of later tradition—to be tolerated as good Catholics. The combination, then, of biblical allegiance, credal orthodoxy, fervent piety, and a reforming spirit—underscored by their persecution by the Roman Catholic Church—qualified these several late medieval movements as "morning stars of the Reformation" and, as such, precursors also of evangelicalism.

Reformers, Puritans, and Pietists

When in 1517 Martin Luther tacked up his theological debating points on the community bulletin board—or, as more recent scholarship suggests, sent his queries to planners of an academic symposium (versus how the movies like to portray it, with Luther thunderously hammering the "95 Theses" into the door of the Wittenberg church)—he thus stood in a heritage of Bible-centered reformers going back at least a couple of centuries. From the work of Luther and many others across Europe, from Poland to the British Isles, the Protestant Reformation emerged to change the entire course of Christianity and, indeed, world history.

The Reformation was not, however, a single bloc carved out of the Roman Catholic Church. It was composed of disparate and not always cooperative movements distinguished by different languages, cultures, interest in Renaissance humanism, levels of respect for Rome, forms of regard for the state, degrees of allegiance toward tradition, doctrines, rituals, and (perhaps most fundamental of all) methods of interpreting and applying the scripture they all revered. The story of the Reformation is normally told in terms of Luther and Lutherans, Calvin and Calvinists, Cranmer and Anglicans, and perhaps Knox and Presbyterians (who, along with the Calvinists, made up the bulk of what is known, a bit confusingly, as the Reformed tradition of the Protestant Reformation). But it was the more radically biblicistic and spiritual impulses, sometimes referred to as primitivism—more typical of lesser lights such as the Swiss Ulrich Zwingli, the Dutch Menno Simons, and the German Caspar Schwenckfeld—that would come to predominate in our time.

So far, however, we have encountered only Christians and then Protestant Christians. Where are the evangelicals?

The Protestants themselves used the term evangelical to describe their fidelity to the gospel over against the ostensible aberrance of their Roman Catholic counterparts. And faithfulness to the gospel was the watchword of subsequent renewal movements in European Christianity as well. As the new boundaries of confessional identity were established in Europe through the turmoil of the late sixteenth and seventeenth centuries, individuals and movements arose to prod the new official Protestant churches themselves into fresh vitality.

Foremost among such individuals were Johan Arndt of Germany and Lewis Bayly of England. In their respective bestselling books, *True Christianity* (1606) and *The Practice of Piety* (1613), they exhorted their fellow Christians to authentic Christian devotion. Furthermore, Arndt influenced the founders of Pietism even as Bayly stirred the hearts of his fellow Puritans. It is out of these two movements in particular that evangelicalism emerged. And it is Pietism as a *renewal* movement and Puritanism as a *reform* movement that provide the two main modes of evangelical life.

Pietism aimed at reviving the dormant flame of Lutheran devotion in the century after the Reformation. The initial tract of Pietism, P. J. Spener's *Pia Desideria*, posed no critique of Lutheran doctrine, Lutheran ritual, or the structure of Lutheran ecclesiastical life (or "polity"). There was no intention to start a new movement, much less a separate denomination. Instead, Spener and his successors—chief among them being pastor and entrepreneur A. H. Francke and biblical scholar J. A. Bengel— wanted merely to rekindle Lutheran spirituality, to warm hearts that had grown lukewarm, or even cool, toward the great truths of the gospel.

To facilitate renewal, Spener did more than just exhort. He suggested changes, most notably the formation of small groups (*ecclesiolae in ecclesia*—"little churches within the church") in which serious-minded Christians could study the Bible, pray, and otherwise encourage each other. These small fires would, Spener hoped, bring light and heat to the church as a whole. And since the gospel is for everyone in every part of life, Pietists founded institutions for the common good, particularly around their center in Halle. They began schools for the rich, the middle-class, and the poor alike, from kindergartens to a university, with trade schools and tutoring for both girls and boys. They also started an orphanage, a farm, and (what for Germans would have been necessary even as it would startle evangelicals of other places and times) a brewery. Pietism, alas, eventually declined from this early balance of head, heart, and hands into an inward religion of strong feeling and little attention to intellectual or social concerns, much to the frustration of later sons of Pietist homes such as Immanuel Kant, Friedrich Schleiermacher, and Friedrich Nietzsche. And it also fairly early diverged into streams beyond Lutheranism, such as the Moravian movement of Count Nicholas von Zinzendorf. This group combined a remnant of the late medieval Hussite movement (followers of Jan Hus) with Pietism to form a new, strongly experiential tradition that would so influence evangelical leader John Wesley. Moravians and Wesley's own group, known as Methodists, in turn eventually inspired the *Réveil*, an early nineteenth-century spiritual movement in French-speaking Switzerland and the borderlands of France that brought fresh spiritual winds into the Reformed tradition there.

Puritanism, by contrast, aimed straightforwardly at changing the Church of England. Its name (originally a derisory epithet) comes from the conviction that the sixteenth-century reformation of the church begun under Tudor monarchs Edward VI and Elizabeth I did not go nearly far enough. Too much Catholicism remained, and the subsequent Stuart kings, James I and Charles I, sounded too much like their respective mother and grandmother, Mary, Queen of Scots, and not enough like her gadfly, the fiery preacher John Knox. Religion and politics being tightly interwoven in the British politics of the seventeenth century—as they are in most places and times—Puritanism became the badge of republicans who deposed and executed Charles I and put Oliver Cromwell in his place. Calvinist doctrine, already influential on the Church of

England's doctrinal statement (the Thirty-Nine Articles) and liturgy (the Book of Common Prayer), could now hold full sway. But in regard to polity and ritual, what of those issues that had divided Protestants from each other since the days of Luther and Calvin a century before?

The Puritans agreed on what they did not want—a temporizing Church of England—but they did not agree on what they did want. And once they were in charge, their differences erupted into fractious competition. Presbyterians wanted churches to be governed by committees of "elders" (Greek *presbuteroi*), while Congregationalists wanted every believer to have a say in churches governed entirely at the local (congregational) level. Baptists agreed with congregationalist polity, but disagreed with Presbyterians and Congregationalists over, yes, baptism. They believed that only people capable of understanding and consenting to the gospel should be baptized, not infants. And the Society of Friends, or Quakers, so recoiled from all things Catholic and emphasized the spiritual nature of the faith so strongly that they abandoned actual water baptism—and, for good measure, the taking of actual bread and wine in communion.

Such a divided house could not stand, and when Cromwell made himself odious by various extreme actions, both in military ruthlessness (especially in Ireland) and in political hegemony (by becoming Lord Protector, a virtual dictatorship), the backlash was severe. Charles II was given the throne and the more visible Puritans fled—mostly to the (Calvinistic) Netherlands, Scotland, or the emerging English colonies of North America.

Puritanism as a broad cultural movement of reformation, therefore, petered out in its British homeland, surviving here and there, especially in circles of Calvinistic Baptists and Methodists, even as it became powerfully formative in the eventual United States of America. But its legacy of intelligent and passionate spiritual writing—from the sermons and treatises of William

Perkins, John Owen, and Richard Baxter to the commentaries of Matthew Henry to the tracts and allegories of John Bunyan—informed and inspired many evangelicals to come. Its anti-Catholicism showed up in the evangelical bloodstream. And the insistence of the Puritans that Christian principles should do more than guide religious life but should also, in at least some concrete way, shape civic life became a theme in evangelical engagement with the world. Not just spiritual and ecclesiastical renewal, therefore, but also cultural reformation were the inheritance of evangelicals from Pietism and Puritanism, an inheritance that resourced a very wide range of implications in the centuries to follow.

The ur-evangelicals

It was a Sunday like any other. The eighteenth-century New England congregation gathered once again to hear their preacher. The young Yale graduate Jonathan Edwards had come to Northampton, Massachusetts, to succeed his grandfather, Solomon Stoddard, who had retired from a long and popular incumbency. Edwards had impressed his flock with his sanctity, rigor, and intelligence, if not his homiletical power. This particular morning, there were no expectations that spiritual lightning would strike. Edwards took his place in the pulpit to preach what would become the most famous sermon in American history, "Sinners in the Hands of an Angry God." And when he concluded—well, it was a Sunday like any other. He quietly greeted parishioners as they exited, and everyone went home to Sunday lunch.

That Sunday was so unremarkable, in fact, that its date is lost to history. But not the morning of July 8, 1741. On that Sunday, Edwards preached at nearby Enfield, Connecticut, to a church that had been previously untouched by the fervor of a "Great Awakening" that had swept through both New England and the Middle Colonies over the previous few years, particularly in 1740 during the triumphant New England tour of the English preacher George Whitefield. Edwards dutifully brought along this sermon he had preached to apparently little effect on his own congregation, only to see the Enfield church catch fire.

As Edwards spoke on the holiness of God, the sinfulness of human beings, and the precarious position above the flames of judgment of everyone who could not claim a lively faith in the salvation God graciously offered all sinners, people moaned aloud. Some even called out as he preached, "What must I do to be saved?" The revival at Enfield became a sensation, and Edwards's sermon was printed soon afterward—to be anthologized in high school textbooks for decades to follow.

Jonathan Edwards, gifted with perhaps the greatest intellect in America at the time, was an outlier when it came to preachers in the Great Awakening. He was not especially talented as a speaker or as a pastor—indeed, the Northampton congregation to which he returned from Enfield with a measure of newfound spiritual authority later turned him out as unendurably strict. Edwards ended up in a frontier church, in the relative quiet of which he turned out some of the most profound works of philosophy, theology, and even psychology ever penned. The Great Awakening itself was not, however, a blossoming of intellectual creativity, but a firestorm of spiritual fervor.

At the center of the conflagration was the firebrand from England, the young George Whitefield. Upsurges of spiritual concern went back to Solomon Stoddard's time and beyond. But it was Whitefield's tours of the colonies, from the Middle Colonies to the South and back up to New England in 1739 and 1740, that both provoked new excitement and connected the various local revivals into America's first national experience.

If Edwards was the extraordinary scholar of emerging evangelicalism, Whitefield was its best spokesman. A friend of the

Wesley brothers at Oxford, he soon became renowned for his dramatic preaching in a time when most pastors carefully wrote out and then read their sermons. Possessed of an unusual talent for drama, he often acted out parts, whether of biblical characters or illustrative figures from contemporary life, to make his homiletical points. David Garrick, the leading actor of the day, once exclaimed, "I would give a hundred guineas if I could say 'O!' like Mr. Whitefield." Perhaps in admiring jest, it was said that Whitefield could move audiences to tears merely by pronouncing the word "Mesopotamia." Even Benjamin Franklin, not known for his evangelical sympathies, became Whitefield's friend, testifying to others that he had to stop himself from reaching into his wallet whenever Whitefield asked audiences to support his orphanage in Georgia. Thus, while Edwards's career spoke to God's inscrutable sovereignty in blessing where and when God willed—an ordinary Sunday in Northampton followed by an extraordinary Sunday in Enfield, under the impress of the very same sermon and preacher—Whitefield's seemed to testify to the power of God-given talent directed to a holy cause: revival. Whether God's work was "surprising," as Edwards put it in one popular account of the awakening, or was to be counted on as the effect of the appropriate means deployed in the appropriate ways was an argument for evangelicals ever after.

John Wesley's career provides grounds to argue both sides of the debate. Raised in a clerical home under the particularly strong influence of his mother, Susanna, Wesley went to Oxford so serious about methodically practicing the Christian faith that the club he joined and soon dominated there was tagged the "Holy Club," "Bible Moths," and, yes, "Methodists." Duly ordained in the Church of England upon graduation, Wesley set sail for the American colonies—only to be discouraged by the indifference of most of his pastoral charges and his own unwisdom in responding to it. Returning by ship to England, he reflected on the behavior of the Moravian Pietists he had witnessed during a life-threatening storm on the outward voyage. While others wailed or cursed, the

Pietists quietly sang hymns, testifying to their faith in God's providence. The young clergyman longed for such assurance, only to receive it when he attended one of their Bible studies in London on May 24, 1738: "In the evening, I went very unwillingly to a society in Aldersgate Street, where one was reading Luther's Preface to the Epistle to the Romans. About a quarter before nine, while he was describing the change which God works in the heart through faith in Christ, I felt my heart strangely warmed. I felt I did trust in Christ, Christ alone for salvation; and an assurance was given me that he had taken away *my* sins, even *mine*, and saved *me* from the law of sin and death."

Because Wesley's life was punctuated by a number of powerful spiritual experiences, scholars over the years have argued over whether this moment was Wesley's definitive "conversion experience" or something else. (He himself skips right over it in the autobiographical portion of his *Plain Account of Christian Perfection*.) The episode was, however, typical of the evangelical conversion experience, and not just because Wesley experienced a warm heart and an assurance of personal salvation. It was also characteristic of the movement Wesley went on to lead that the experience happened in a small group studying the Bible, not at a big preaching service commanded by the likes of Whitefield. (Indeed, his brother Charles, also an Anglican clergyman, had undergone a strikingly similar set of experiences three days earlier.)

Wesley himself was a successful preacher, traversing Britain indefatigably over the next decades. Reliable estimates put Wesley's travels at a quarter of a million miles on horseback as he preached 800 sermons a year to crowds as large as 20,000. But he concluded after witnessing a number of apparently fruitful preaching occasions soon dying on the vine that he would not preach anywhere he could not also set up small groups. If Edwards was the brilliant intellectual light of early evangelicalism and Whitefield its consummate fire starter, Wesley was its

2. John Wesley faces a mob at Wednesbury, England (1743), as he preached in public spaces when pulpits were closed to his message of an instant New Birth.

organizational genius. He devised a group or two for every sort of person, from initial inquirers to veteran believers, designed to build fireplaces in which the Spirit could blaze helpfully at length—without setting alight too many unstable folk whose excesses brought ignominy to revivalism. In this project he followed in the train of the Pietists and, indeed, of the Puritans, who also had formed small societies or "covenanted groups" for mutual support.

Edwards, Whitefield, and Wesley would have been standouts in any age. Evangelicalism took shape and took flight in this era also, however, because of its strong supporting cast. Selina Hastings, Countess of Huntingdon, used her wealth and influence to support with education and wages those following in Whitefield's train as revivalist preachers. And her participation meant that it was harder to write off the evangelicals as mere "enthusiasts," a term of anxious contempt recalling the worst of the seventeenth-century religious extremes, when people of her social status were patrons. London printer John Lewis was the movement's first historian and Scot John Gillies tirelessly promoted awakening as Whitefield's official biographer and custodian of his literary legacy. Charles Wesley, John's younger brother and a fellow cleric, theologically directed and immeasurably boosted the power of not only the Methodists but also many other evangelical movements by writing hymn lyrics of unsurpassed clarity and richness. (Indeed, Charles is easily the world's most popular hymnwriter to this day.)

What, however, connected a spiritual outbreak in New England, an American preaching tour by a traveling Englishman, and a British network of small societies—beyond, perhaps, a common love for Charles Wesley's hymns? Skeptical historians ask whether there is a "something" here to be discerned, a coherent happening we can study in hopes of finding nascent evangelicalism.

The participants themselves said that they recognized in each other a common focus on revival, literally "new life"—or, as they put it in terms of John 3, "New Birth." They opposed the formal, "automatic" nature of state-church Christianity, the assumption that anyone who was not clearly non-Christian (Jews, Romani, visitors or merchants from faraway places) would be baptized as an infant and raised as a Christian. Authentic Christianity—and these people were big on adjectives such as *authentic, real, genuine, true,* and the like—is not merely a matter of outward conformity to social norms. Real Christianity is fundamentally a matter of encountering God literally in a spiritual way: becoming aware of and repentant for one's sin; trusting God to save oneself from hell through the substitutionary penalty paid by Christ on the Cross; committing oneself to discipleship to the risen Lord Jesus; cooperating with the rehabilitative and maturing work of the Holy Spirit in one's heart; and sharing the good news of salvation with others, in both word and deed.

For evangelicals, genuine Christianity therefore is focused on the evangel, purified from ecclesiastical and social errors, and gratefully dutiful in obeying, and extending the influence of, the Word of God. Edwards, Whitefield, and the Wesleys recognized the same concerns and outcomes in each other's work and typically, if not invariably, commended each other as godly fellow workers even across differences of denomination, theology, and more. Indeed, a lively transatlantic correspondence, both in private letters and in publications, sprang up in the eighteenth century to promote this "season" of God's blessing throughout the Anglosphere—and beyond into the European regions touched by Pietism (mostly middle European and eventually Scandinavian) and the French Huguenot (Calvinist) movement.

Did all of these particular instances of revival, however, constitute a connected movement? They were quite diverse in denomination, location, and social station. The earliest outbreaks in America were in the 1720s and 1730s under the preaching of Theodore Frelinghuysen, a German American preacher in the Dutch Reformed tradition working in New Jersey, and under the ministry of the Tennent family, who were Scots Irish Presbyterian immigrants to Pennsylvania. Edwards was of Puritan stock and his own congregation in Northampton, Massachusetts, experienced a "surprising" work of God in the 1730s (some years before he preached that incendiary sermon in Enfield, Connecticut). George Whitefield and the Wesley brothers, by contrast, were Englishmen ordained in the Church of England, and the Methodist movement was always intended to remain a force for renewal within that church (as Pietism was within Lutheranism), not a separate denomination. Meanwhile, revivals had broken out separately in Wales, notably under the preaching of Howell Harris, and in Scotland, too, not only through the tours of John Wesley and especially of Whitefield, but also through the ministry of Scots Presbyterian pastors, notably from the family Erskine. On the more radical fringes, moreover, Baptists and even Quakers were touched with evangelical fervor.

As similar in tone and appearance as were all these awakenings—such that the caricatures of William Hogarth could be understood to depict scenes virtually anywhere among them—the question remains as to whether they cohered into an actual movement. Leaders did correspond and occasionally work together. They eagerly shared news. Many did testify to the sense that this was indeed a single, sustained outbreak of God's blessing that might result in the evangelization of the whole world and the subsequent soon return of Jesus Christ.

The historian looks in vain, however, for large-scale joint projects mounted by joint institutions. Indeed, unlike the Puritans and Pietists before them, these early reformers focused entirely on spiritual matters, leaving social reform largely to other people on other days. A cooperative spirit among them was evident, but the record contains few instances of actual cooperation beyond mutual encouragement. What united these various outbreaks of revival was largely a common message and a common mode celebrated in mutually encouraging correspondence and journalism—along with the peripatetic figure of Whitefield plus the widely loved hymns of Charles Wesley. Does that amount to a historical something, a new phenomenon we can point to and call evangelicalism?

Chapter 2
Evangelicalism defined

The term *evangelicalism* derives from the Greek word *euaggelion*, Latinized to *evangelium*, which means "good news." In older English, *good news* is "godspell," which eventually gives us "gospel." And for Christians the gospel is the good news of God saving the world, particularly through the inspiring and instructive career, the atoning suffering and death, and the promissory resurrection and ascension of Jesus Christ; the converting work of the Holy Spirit; and the eventual return of Christ to earth to finally set all to rights.

Thus the adjective evangelical means "of or pertaining to the good news." It becomes a badge of honor in church history: a declaration of authenticity particularly in contrast to false, hollow, or inert versions of the faith. The medieval saint Francis of Assisi was thus sometimes referred to as evangelical to affirm the ethos of his work over against the venal, or political, or merely formal Christianity of his contemporaries.

Francis was also an evangelist. This noun signifies someone who spreads the good news. In that sense, every genuine Christian is an evangelist, since all are called to share their faith with others, per Christ's Great Commission to his first disciples (Matt. 28:18–20). But the Apostle Paul also speaks of those who are gifted by the Holy Spirit to declare the gospel with unusual effectiveness, just as other Christians are unusually good at teaching, or leading, or showing hospitality (Eph. 4:11–12). George Whitefield is a fine example of an evangelist among the evangelicals.

It was not until the Protestant Reformation that evangelical as a noun came into wide use to denote the genuine Christians (the Protestants) in contrast to those ostensibly still captive to the encrustations of the Middle Ages, the Roman Catholics. Evangelical thus becomes a word of self-congratulation marking out Protestants over against Catholics, as it does in German to this day: *evangelisch*.

What, then, is distinctive about the so-called evangelicals of the eighteenth-century revivals? We have traced their descent from certain movements in late medieval piety (the Waldensians, the Lollards, and the Hussites) through the Protestant Reformation and then via both the continental renewal movement of Pietism and the British reform movement of Puritanism. When we arrive at the Wesleys, Whitefield, Edwards, and the rest, at what or whom have we arrived?

Three options face us. The first is to view evangelicalism the way that many evangelicals themselves see it, as denoting the true faith. One of the twentieth century's leading evangelicals, the English pastor and author John R. W. Stott, titled his bestselling treatment of evangelical theology simply *Basic Christianity* (1958). This definition, however, is problematic for observers who want to avoid picking sides in ecclesiastical conflicts: scholars, jurists, journalists, politicians, and more.

The second option is to view evangelicalism as a movement: a coherent historical phenomenon, individuals and institutions both united in conviction and mission and organized in cooperative work toward shared goals. This vision animated various attempts at evangelical ecumenism: from the Evangelical Alliance (founded in 1846), through the World Missionary Conference in Edinburgh (1910), through the national fellowships of evangelicals (such as the National Association of Evangelicals in the United States, 1942; the Evangelical Fellowship of Canada, 1964; and counterparts around the world), through various special-purpose groups (such as the Student Volunteer Movement, Youth with a Mission, and Compassion); and the revival of global connections in the World Evangelical Fellowship (1951; renamed the World Evangelical Alliance in 2001). The ideal of a "united evangelical front" to represent common concerns to government and to advance the gospel together has long prompted evangelicals to see themselves as connected in a joint endeavor.

Alas, for this vision, however, it claims both too much and too little. The formal membership of these organizations has often not included significant Protestant bodies that would seem congenial to their concerns. Various Lutheran, Reformed, and even Baptist groups have kept to themselves. Furthermore, self-identified evangelical fellowships have only sometimes included the many like-minded Christians in denominations not typically identified as evangelical, especially state churches and large pluralized denominations such as the Church of England or the United Methodist Church. Even in cooperative events and within the same country, new groups such as the Pentecostal churches (a particularly exuberant form of evangelicalism emphasizing spectacular spiritual gifts, notably healing and speaking in spiritual languages) could be included in one place (such as the Billy Graham evangelistic campaign in Melbourne in 1959) and excluded in others (such as the campaign that followed it in Sydney later that same year).

Even the ur-evangelicals were not bound together in common organizations. Outside the multiple structures of Wesley's Methodism—with its groupings into various "classes" and "societies" of Christians at various stages of spiritual maturity that extended from local to regional and even national levels—revivals tended to be local and to spread through existing networks of denominational, geographical, and personal links. Evangelicals gladly read of similar occasions of renewal across the English-speaking world and beyond. But these scattered flare-ups over most of the eighteenth century do not connect into a single conflagration.

A third option thus commends itself: evangelicalism as a style. One might see Christianity in the modern era occurring in three main styles: a conscientious maintenance of the past, a determined freedom toward the present and future, and a way between the two.

Conservatism concerns itself with preserving the heritage handed down from the past. Doctrines, rites, mores, polities—all are received from one's forebears as a sacred trust to be transferred as faithfully as possible unto succeeding generations in perpetuity. Conservatism thus varies per the tradition in question. Roman Catholic traditionalism will differ hugely from, say, Baptist or Presbyterian or Greek Orthodox traditionalism, even as they will differ from each other. But the dynamic remains the same: conservation of the legacy.

Liberalism, by contrast, receives the tradition and then does as it thinks best with it in the light of what else Christians are experiencing and learning today. *Liber* means "free," and liberalism freely adds to, subtracts from, and modifies whatever it continues to esteem from the past. Liberal Catholics, then, can be presumed to practice at least a somewhat different form of Christianity than will liberal Protestants or Orthodox. In any given society, however, the pressure of the dominant cultural consensus may make them more alike than one might anticipate. Indeed, liberals across denominational and even religious lines will resemble each other in any given cultural situation—such as, say, liberal Catholics, Protestants, Jews, and Muslims in New York, Paris, or Sydney.

Evangelicalism, then, is the third way—at least, it is the Protestant version of this third way. (The mainstream of evangelicalism has always understood itself as Protestant and I shall respect that tradition here, thus leaving it to others to characterize this third mode for Catholic, Orthodox, and other Christians.) Evangelicalism is not merely a transmitter of the tradition, however loyal it considers itself to be toward "the faith once and for all delivered to the saints" (Jude 1:3). Evangelicals feel free to appropriate the tradition selectively in terms of what they see to be the core of Christianity and then innovate as necessary in order to fulfill their mission. But evangelicalism is indeed anchored in the tradition, and especially in the sacred text at the heart of that tradition, the Bible. Evangelicalism's identity is that of "basic Christianity," so evangelicals deviate from the past only in the name of what they understand to be the best principles of the past. They attempt to construe and to practice Christianity in the creative tension between the heritage they inherit and the challenges they now face. This style of modern Christianity has a distinctive shape that proceeds from the eighteenth century until now.

Definition

Who are the evangelicals? What do they characteristically care about, and what do they typically do?

"Everything should be made as simple as possible," Albert Einstein is said to have said, "but no simpler." We will work with six characteristics of evangelicals, even as we will have to split each of those six into two divisions . . . and then complicate things a bit more for some of those divisions as well. The divisions and complications are necessary to ensure that the definition truly denotes evangelicalism and not a larger entity such as Protestantism or even Christianity itself. Here, then, is a list of key adjectives to define evangelicalism: Trinitarian, biblicist, conversionist, missional, populist, and pragmatic.

Trinitarian

Evangelicals emphasize the three persons of the Christian Godhead: Father, Son, and Holy Spirit. As in the New Testament itself, God the Father and Jesus Christ occupy the foreground. But the Holy Spirit is irreducibly key to evangelicalism as well.

Taking Jesus first, evangelicals emphasize that Jesus is Savior and Lord. As Savior in his first advent, Jesus announced the good news that God's Kingdom was now present (in himself), not merely to be hoped for in the future. Jesus modeled as the Son of Man how to live in the light of that incoming Kingdom. Jesus taught the way of life of the life to come. He then suffered and died for the sins of a world of sinners who deserve to suffer and die for our sins. And in his Second Coming, Jesus will reappear as Savior to rescue the faithful, judge the resistant, and usher in the delights of the everlasting world to come.

As Lord, risen from the dead and ascended to the right hand of God the Father, Jesus presides over the church. He directs the church in all it is to do and supplies the resources the church needs to fulfill its calling. As Lord, he also governs the world, contending with the forces of evil and bending them to his sovereign will such that the course of history goes his way, ultimately resulting in the fulfillment of God's plan of global salvation. As the definitive revelation of God, therefore, and as the agent at the center of the inauguration of the Kingdom, the atonement for sin, and the new regime to come, Jesus naturally garners the most attention from evangelicals. Evangelical sermons, hymns, art, and piety all focus on Jesus.

The Holy Spirit, nonetheless, figures importantly in evangelical thought and life. The Nicene Creed describes the Holy Spirit as "the Giver of Life," and evangelicals take that truth seriously. It is the work of the Holy Spirit, after all, to bring to each believer a new birth, a spiritual renewal from the deadness of sin to become alive to God. To be "born again" is the quintessential evangelical testimony, and this work of regeneration (to use the technical theological term) is the province of the third Person of the Trinity. It is the work of the Holy Spirit, then, to take each new believer and rehabilitate him or her: to purify each person from sin and to train each Christian in holiness so that he or she eventually will be fit to live in the glorious world to come. This is the work of sanctification, helping believers become progressively more and more fully dedicated to God.

It is not enough, therefore, to describe evangelicals only by way of devotion to Jesus, much less even more narrowly in terms of focusing on his Cross—as many observers have done heretofore. Jesus accomplished and accomplishes far more than atoning for sin, in both evangelical doctrine and evangelical piety. And salvation is far more than what Jesus does, but what the whole Trinity effects, particularly via the Holy Spirit.

Moreover, evangelicalism does not have to wait for the twentieth-century Pentecostal movement to rediscover the third Person of the Trinity. He is everywhere in the letters, sermons, devotional guides, and hymns of the ur-evangelicals themselves. George Whitefield was transformed into a preaching powerhouse after he read Scottish Presbyterian Henry Scougal's great tract, *The Life of God in the Soul of Man* (1677), a book that introduced him to a personal, immediate relationship with God in the Spirit. He made his own views clear in *The Indwelling of the Spirit, the Common Privilege of All Believers* (1739). One of Jonathan Edwards's most important reflections on revival explicitly credits the Holy Spirit: *Distinguishing Marks of a Work of the Spirit of God* (1741). Charles Wesley extols the Holy Spirit often in his 6,000 hymns and poems:

> The gift unspeakable sent down,
>   The Spirit of life, and power, and love.
> Send us the Spirit of thy Son

To make the depths of Godhead known,
   To make us share the life divine;
Send him the sprinkled blood t'apply,
Send him our souls to sanctify,
   And show and seal us ever thine.
   ("Father of Everlasting Grace," 1742)

And "grace" is virtually a metonym for the Holy Spirit in what is nowadays the most familiar of evangelical hymns, John Newton's "Amazing Grace." Evangelicals thus are not just "Jesus people," but fully Trinitarian.

Biblicist

Evangelicals love the Bible. And they love it in at least two main ways. First, the Bible is typically touted by evangelicals as their supreme authority for the faithful Christian life. The Bible tells evangelicals the gospel, and it tells them how to live in the light of the gospel. The leading evangelical writers in every age, perhaps particularly in their polemics when they have aimed to be as persuasive as possible, have drawn not only on scripture but also on quotations from eminent historical figures, philosophical maxims, the ancient creeds, historical parallels, contemporary scholarship, evocative poetry, and more. Wesley and Edwards readily commended the findings of modern science, especially medicine, to their followers as gifts also of God. When it has come to the basic content of their faith and to the adjudication of conflicts about the faith, however, evangelicals have eschewed mysticism, rationalism, traditionalism, or any sort of teaching authority (such as a pope or church council) for an unapologetic submission to the Bible. "The Bible says it; I believe it; that settles it" is merely the popular evangelical version of the Reformation slogan "*Sola scriptura*" (only scripture). Careful evangelicals, moreover, will add to any affirmation of the authority of the Bible a crucial qualifier such as this: "as interpreted properly under the

27

3. The peoples of polar North America receive a Bible in Inuktitut. Evangelicals have been in the forefront not only of Bible translation, but in the reduction of oral languages to writing and in the preservation of native languages.

guidance of the Holy Spirit," thus underlining the importance of the Holy Spirit in yet another role.

This allegiance to the Bible as supreme and unparalleled authority helps to mark off evangelicalism as Protestant. So does evangelical insistence that atonement for sin was entirely accomplished in the Cross of Christ. And evangelical refusal to defer to papal authority and to the self-understanding of the Roman Catholicism as the one true church, preferring instead an ecclesiology marked by both pragmatism and populism, makes all the more clear the Protestant ethos of evangelicalism. Polls that purport to find evangelicals among Roman Catholics, and perhaps also among the Orthodox, either are not using correct and sufficient criteria or are finding de facto crypto-Protestants.

Such convictions do not entail anti-intellectualism, as if evangelicals all restrict their search for truth to a Spirit-guided study of scripture alone. Jonathan Edwards was broadly conversant in a handful of disciplines, from biology to psychology to philosophy to theology to ethics. John Wesley not only was remarkably erudite, but also edited a library of books to be read by his thousands of followers, from medical counsel to mystical musings. To be sure, evangelical deference to the Bible became for many evangelicals a naive biblicism that interfered with, and even substituted for, a proper appreciation and practice of scholarship. For an analysis of current political events, for example, many evangelicals, led by certain enthusiastic but uninformed preachers, looked only to prophetic scripture as their interpretative key instead of to history and what would become the social sciences. The more learned evangelicals, however, have looked to both kinds of resources and integrate them in a single Christian worldview, as both Wesley and Edwards did in their day.

This devotion to the Bible without a corresponding devotion to tradition and an authoritative ecclesiastical arbitrator has been derided as resulting in what one critic refers to as "pervasive interpretive pluralism." With Protestant denominations numbering close to 50,000 around the world, no one can doubt that there is substantial diversity in evangelical ranks. Yet the ur-evangelicals had no trouble recognizing what they saw as authentic Christian piety among Protestants of various denominations—and even, for some large-minded evangelicals such as John Wesley and George Whitefield, among Roman Catholics. And what they recognized was recognizably the same basic doctrine and narrative of God reconciling the world to himself in Jesus (2 Cor. 5:19), just as it remains recognizably the same among evangelicals in subsequent centuries. There simply is not "pervasive interpretive pluralism" among evangelicals such that they cannot agree on the essentials of the faith enough to cooperate in a very wide range of shared endeavors, from relief agencies to youth camps to even theological seminaries.

The Bible also functions as the center of evangelical piety. Because evangelicals can be found in such a wide range of denominations, generalizing about evangelical church experience is difficult. But walk into the main meeting room of an evangelical church and you will almost certainly see a pulpit front and center. The preaching of scripture has long been the focal point of the typical evangelical worship service, while in other groups the symbolic altar on which sit the bread and wine of the Lord's Supper is central, because taking communion together is the high point of the meeting. The hymns and songs sung before and after the sermon will have been either based on scriptural teaching or themselves pastiches of scriptural phrases. Look around on a Sunday morning and you will see believers with personal copies of the Bible in hand, and likely those Bibles will be open during the sermon, perhaps accompanied by a notebook in which to capture important teachings (while younger members might be thumbing notes into their phones).

In an evangelical home there will be multiple Bibles, at least one for each member of the family. In fact, the marketing of various kinds of Bibles, in a range of covers, sizes, and typefaces, goes back to the mid-nineteenth century. In even earlier generations, there would be at least a grand family Bible in a position of honor on a prominent shelf, to be read during weekly or even daily family devotions. And, as was true of Christians in other traditions, in the pages of this Bible important family events (births, marriages, deaths) would be recorded, since it was the center of family life and the heirloom most likely to be passed down through the generations.

Evangelicals produced and consumed a substantial material culture. By the nineteenth century, evangelicals were enjoying graphic renditions of scripture texts and other inspirational quotations on their walls and tea and coffee sets decorated with Bible scenes on their parlor tables. The twentieth century gave evangelicals distinctive art, from Warner Sallman's massively popular "Head of Christ" (1940) to Thomas Kinkade's widely marketed landscapes of heavenly repose a generation later. And for several decades (until the rise of Amazon), so-called Bible bookstores offered up a bazaar of household items—from keychains to greeting cards to the inevitable T-shirts to cartoon videos for the kids—replete with evangelical edification. But for all the "Jesus junk" they carried, the stores were still Bible bookstores. The Bible continued to be the touchstone of evangelical piety.

Evangelicals characteristically have memorized scripture, so much so that everyday conversation and correspondence are sprinkled with biblical phrases—even jokes might assume a common knowledge of the text. Guidance from God, especially in moments of special stress, is sought in prayer, but also in the pages of the Bible: sometimes in a magical way, with an apparently random text suddenly glowing with pertinence, but more commonly in a straightforward sense, with a relevant biblical teaching coming to mind or being intentionally consulted. The Bible therefore truly has functioned at the center of evangelical Christianity.

Conversionist

If evangelicals are generally known for anything, it is for conversion, the change from one spiritual state to another. But two pairs of concepts are critical to the evangelical understanding of conversion.

First, evangelicals believe not only that one must be born again, but also that one must then grow up to become a mature believer. Evangelicals generally have been fiercely against "antinomianism," the idea that because God has "saved" you, you can now do anything you like without regard for the law (*nomos*) of God. Instead, evangelicals have taught that while entry into God's adoptive family is truly free—all you have to do is willingly join—the obligations of familyhood are total. One is obliged to behave now like a child of God, and one embarks on a lifelong

31

regimen under the tutelage of the Holy Spirit to become a consistently dedicated (= "holy") child of God. Evangelical conversion thus includes both regeneration and sanctification.

The stereotype of the dramatic one-time conversion experience does hold for many, but not all, evangelicals. Evangelicals in pedobaptist traditions (those who baptize infants of believing parents) tend to emphasize the process of sanctification, while believers' baptist traditions (those who baptize those old enough to declare faith for themselves) tend to emphasize the moment of regeneration, becoming born again. Evangelicals of both traditions, however, agree with the general Christian teaching of original sin, that each person is born with a moral deficit from which the Holy Spirit must rescue, renew, and rehabilitate the person. And evangelicals all agree that merely being born again is not enough; maturation is required to enter the world to come. Indeed, the great twentieth-century American evangelist Billy Graham, world renowned for inviting people to become born again at one of his meetings, recognized that some believers do not recall a single dramatic conversion experience. (His mother and his wife were examples to him of indubitably genuine Christians who nonetheless could not point to a single moment of decision for Christ.) The heart of evangelicalism was appropriation: Were you *now* truly following Jesus, trusting God for salvation and cooperating with the Holy Spirit in his sanctifying work? If not, then you should come to Christ. If so, then you need not fret if you had no dramatic conversion story to tell.

Indeed, the question of assurance has loomed large in evangelical history, but not as univocally as some preachers and some later interpreters have suggested. It is true that the ur-evangelicals typically emphasized that one could know right here and now that one was truly a Christian, made right with God by the Holy Spirit. To discern this fact, the Puritans had devoted many hours, extending over years, of introspection and inspection of the moral pattern of their lives. But through the immediate testimony of the Spirit in one's heart and the clear promises of scripture in one's mind, evangelicals could know it now.

Several attendant questions, however, were championed by certain evangelicals to the consternation of others. Some later evangelicals would go on to distrust the feelings of the heart as dangerous enthusiasm. So they reduced assurance to a cognitive recognition of the substance and truth of the gospel promise in the divine decree of salvation. In Wesley's own day, he and his fellow Arminians (notably his friend and defender John Fletcher) so fretted about antinomianism—a desultory complacency about moral rectitude stemming from a blanket assurance of certain salvation offered by certain Calvinists—that they fervently warned believers to avoid forfeiting their salvation. And since John Wesley himself testified to multiple experiences of worry followed by moments of fresh conviction, it was not obvious to all just what sort of assurance was on offer and could be expected. So while evangelicals did indeed preach assurance, they did so in enough different ways and with enough different qualifications to defy listing it as a characteristic conviction.

The second element of conversion for evangelicals is not only for individuals, but also for groups and communities. God is saving each person one by one, but also adopting believers into God's global family of faith. The *corporate* dimension of conversion, furthermore, is to be sought for both church and society, and evangelicals have typically been busy both planting and renewing churches, on the one hand, and seeking moral and spiritual progress in society at large on the other.

Missional

Evangelicals are known for evangelism. Because evangelicals have been committed to sanctification, however, they have poured resources also into the education of their youth in Sunday schools, evangelical elementary and secondary schools, boys and girls clubs, summer camps, university campus ministries and evangelical colleges, and more. Evangelicals, particularly through large and well-funded Bible societies around the world and through such global ventures as the Summer Institute of Linguistics (now SIL International, founded in 1934) and its sister organization, Wycliffe Bible Translators (1942), have promoted the translation of the Bible into most of the world's languages, thereby fostering widespread literacy. In fact, missionary translators often have been the first to reduce a culture's oral language to writing. Evangelical publishing houses have turned out literature to equip Christians both for the life of faith and for the challenges of public life. Small groups and house churches have sprung up around the world as centers of lay education, mutual support, and worship.

Evangelicals have pursued their mission from God beyond the confines of their own communities. Some have followed Jesus's example of ministering to the poor, the sick, and the outcast, thus demonstrating the comprehensive scope of God's saving work. Others have heeded God's original instructions in the Garden of Eden to care properly for creation and all of their neighbors in it through education for all ages and both sexes, instruction and investment in farms and businesses, advocacy for human rights, campaigns against human trafficking, and, increasingly, global climate change.

Over the centuries, and with accelerating force and extent, evangelicals have founded a startling array of special-purpose groups to foster evangelism, discipleship, and service. Even as modern states have taken over some of the classic Christian charitable functions in healthcare, poverty relief, and education, evangelicals have begun organizations as specialized as Christian adoption agencies and as vast as World Vision and the Salvation Army. In many parts of the world in the twenty-first century, as was true a hundred years ago in many Western cities, an evangelical can participate in not only a local church, but also a businessperson's fellowship, a food bank, an overnight shelter, a school, a clinic, a kids' club, a sewing circle, a missionary support group, and a marriage seminar. Charles Wesley's lyric nicely portrays evangelical activism: "With us no melancholy void, / No period lingers unemployed / Or unimproved below." His brother was more blunt: "Lose no opportunity of doing good in any kind. Be zealous of good works; willingly omit no work, neither of piety or mercy. Do all the good you possibly can to the bodies and souls of men.... Be *active*" (emphasis in original). And all of this busyness for God had evangelistic import, as Charles concludes: "Thus may I show thy Spirit within /... The truth of my religion prove / By perfect purity and love."

Populist

To the foregoing familiar traits of evangelicals we must add this fifth one. By this term is meant both a *legitimation* and a *mode*. In evangelical terms, this appeal to the masses is justified in terms of the Reformation doctrine of "the priesthood of all believers." Originally this phrase was meant narrowly by Martin Luther to denote the spiritual qualification of each believer to hear another's repentance and to console such penitents with the Word of the gospel. (One therefore did not have to restrict auricular confession to a priest.) In subsequent centuries, however, the phrase took on the sense of a broad spiritual competency in the heart of each believer. Since the Holy Spirit dwells in every Christian and since all vocations are blessed by God (and not just the full-time religious), evangelicals typically have concluded that each person not only must decide for himself or herself on Christian matters, but also is fully competent to do so. Gifted teachers have their role to play, but the question of *which* teacher one should attend to in a marketplace of contrasting and even conflicting voices is to be decided by the individual believer. Thus evangelicalism has grown significantly in the context of the modern impulses toward democracy, individualism, and consumerism.

4. The Salvation Army "lassies" gave evangelical charity an appealing face.

Leaders and institutions, doctrines and mores, policies and projects—all are legitimated by popular appeal. Deference is withheld from those who enjoy mere ecclesiastical rank or academic attainment. Theological and ethical wisdom can come from a university-trained pastor, but also from a charismatic farmer-preacher, a young Pentecostal oracle, or a blogger gifted with unusual empathy and winsome prose. Evangelical pastors are acclaimed by a single criterion: not the number of books authored, not the number of missionaries their churches have sent out, not the various ministries their churches offer to their communities, but the number of people in their audiences.

The dominant *mode* of evangelical culture, furthermore, is populist. The music of evangelicalism progressed from the accessible but careful lyrics of Isaac Watts and William Cowper through the moving simplicity of Negro spirituals to the sentimental songs of Fanny Crosby and Philip Bliss in the nineteenth century. It broadened out to the catchy jingles of Ira Sankey and Charlie Alexander, the upbeat joy of gospel music, and the twentieth-century adaptation of almost all forms of popular song into so-called CCM: contemporary Christian music—despite the rearguard campaigns of conservative preachers and parents against "worldly music" (that go back at least as far as the nineteenth century). The best-known evangelical preachers have not been paragons of erudition and eloquence, but plain spoken, vivid, humorous, and focused on stimulating the feelings. Indeed, the preaching ideal down the centuries derives from Whitefield's dramatic example by way of Edwards's concern to stimulate the congregant's *affections* (convictions, motivations), not just teach the doctrines. The architecture of evangelical churches likewise has aimed at mass appeal. In the nineteenth century, it was clearly class based: grand Gothic or Romanesque or Palladian piles testified to the growing cultural status of Methodists and Baptists in rising towns and cities, while congregations serving other constituencies occupied modest chapels and even storefronts. In the twentieth century, the paradigm shifted to generic auditoriums, indistinguishable from secular concert halls or multipurpose rooms in community centers. The American pastor Joel Osteen nicely exemplified these traits via his bestselling books and popular broadcasts around the world stemming from his Houston church housed in a former professional basketball arena.

It is too easy, and too jaundiced, to view all this populism as merely a selling out to rank popularity. Populism makes religious sense given the evangelical confidence that each believer is Spirit filled and thus competent to judge. *Voluntaryism* and *individualism* thus come together in evangelicalism's assumption that, given a genuine allegiance to the faith, the mass approval of all these individuals listening to the Lord is tantamount to divine approval.

Decisions therefore typically have been made by evangelical leaders in terms of what will best garner popular approval, rather than what is most consistent with their heritage (conservatism) or what is most compatible with the best of contemporary learning (liberalism). And populism explains the paradox of such an individualistic movement nonetheless frequently generating authoritarian leaders. For once leaders gain popular approval, they command unquestioned authority as ipso facto God's man or woman—unless they dramatically forfeit it in manifest sin. In evangelicalism, *vox populi, vox Dei*.

Pragmatism

Finally, we encounter evangelicals' concern to get things done. Here is where the conversionist, the missional, and the populist qualities of evangelicalism combine into a driving pragmatic force that shows up particularly in two ways: *transdenominationalism* and *adaptation*.

In the eighteenth-century revivals, there were tensions over doctrine, to be sure, particularly along the fault line of God's sovereign will versus the human capacity to cooperate with God that separated Calvinists from Arminians—a bone of contention that would never disappear. John Wesley and George Whitefield endured a falling-out over such issues that lasted years, and while they eventually reconciled, that controversy flared to life again after Whitefield's death.

Then the rise of premillennial eschatology in the nineteenth century challenged the more optimistic postmillennialism typical of the ur-evangelicals and the amillennialism typical of the wider church. By the twentieth century, premillennialism had become simply normative for most evangelicals, most often in the form of dispensationalism. This latter was a theological scheme developed in the 1830s among the Anglo-Irish Plymouth Brethren and popularized greatly by the Scofield Reference Bible (1909), which published dispensational study notes on the same pages as the sacred text—an innovation that led many untutored readers to regard the notes themselves as inspired. Dispensationalism's sensational reading of end-times prophecy fueled evangelical chiliasm especially in North America, but also around the world, cresting first in Hal Lindsey's *The Late, Great Planet Earth*, the bestselling book of the 1970s in the United States, and then in the popular *Left Behind* novels (and film adaptations) of Tim LaHaye and Jerry Jenkins two decades later. Thus evangelicalism in many locales became identified with dispensational premillennialism even as evangelicals of rival eschatologies contended for their legitimacy.

Stereotypes persisted even in scholarly accounts that far-thinking postmillennials tended to undertake long-term projects of cultural transformation while anxious premillennials tended to scorn social involvement to get as many souls saved as possible before Jesus returned. The record shows, however, that evangelicals all have manifested basically the same character and have gone about basically the same wide range of work, whatever their particular construal of the Second Coming.

Generally, therefore, evangelical Presbyterians recognized the Spirit of God working among evangelical Congregationalists, or

Evangelicalism defined

Baptists, or Anglicans, or Pietists. George Whitefield himself once declared, "I saw regenerate souls among the Baptists, among the Presbyterians, among the Independents, and among the Church [that is, Anglican] folks—all children of God, and yet all born again in a different way of worship: and who can tell which is the most evangelical?" In this openness Whitefield followed in the train of August Hermann Franke of the German Pietists who enjoyed a warm correspondence about missions with Cotton Mather of the New England Puritans, among many others of various stripes. This mutual recognition extended not only to the celebration (in magazines, books, and correspondence) of what God was doing in other denominations, but also to occasional joint action: sponsoring a local preaching visit by George Whitefield in the eighteenth century, for instance, or participating in Keswick spirituality conferences in the nineteenth, or "marching for Jesus" in city streets in the later twentieth.

This was *transdenominationalism*: not the setting aside of denominations (*nondenominationalism*) or the official cooperation of denominations (*interdenominationalism*), but recognition of denominational differences without those differences impeding mutual support and joint action. For if the gospel was to advance most effectively, evangelicals would overlook previously divisive concerns to insist only on the core of doctrine around that gospel and work with anyone who would join that mission. Indeed, the Evangelical Alliance of 1846 acknowledged the truth of the warning issued by the great Scottish preacher and church leader Thomas Chalmers: believers could "think alike" and "feel alike," but they might not "explain alike." By the time the dust settled on that first meeting in London, the statement of faith hammered out by the delegates was not a rigid canon of membership, but only "an indication of the class of persons whom it is desirable to embrace within the Alliance."

Adaptation is the other implication of evangelical pragmatism. "Conservative" should not be used, therefore, as a synonym for evangelical. *Conservative* churches are conservative. Evangelicals, by contrast, have been only *selectively* conservative. Despite stereotypes and, indeed, many congregations to the contrary, they do not characteristically insist that we keep doing as we always have. Instead, many evangelicals have also been progressive, and sometimes even radical—in doctrine, in ethics, in politics, in art, and more: whatever gets the job done. Evangelicals have been quick to adopt new styles and even locales of preaching, new forms of mass media, new polities, new architectures, new types of missions, and more. John Wesley defended the significant deviancy of his movement thus: "We have out of necessity varied [from the Church of England] in some points of discipline, by preaching in the field, by extempore prayer, by employing lay preachers, by forming and regulating [our own] societies, and by holding yearly conferences. But we did none of these things until we were convinced we could no longer omit them but at peril of our souls"—and, he doubtless implied, at the peril of souls we are intent on saving.

It was the Oxford-educated Wesley, in fact, who came to bless and commission poorly educated preachers who would nonetheless tirelessly ride circuits of tiny congregations and preaching stations both in Britain and especially on the North American frontier. Wesley admonished them to read and to cultivate literacy especially for Bible study among their flock. But the needs of the deprived manifestly outweighed and outpaced the tradition of the genteel parson. Farmer-preachers soon arose among the Baptists, the Churches of Christ, and other nineteenth-century denominations who reached thousands, even millions, on the frontier in advance of ecclesiastical systems insistent on university- or seminary-trained pastors. Likewise, evangelicals deployed preachers, well educated or not, among the burgeoning urban poor whose concentrated numbers defied traditional parish systems of ecclesiastical organization.

In the realm of mission, evangelicals have been paradoxically pragmatic about their number one technology: the Bible.

Evangelicals have been known for defending a "high" view of scripture—some of them so devoted to the idea of divine inspiration that the Evangelical Theological Society in the United States traditionally had only one clause in its entire statement of faith required for membership: "The Bible alone, and the Bible in its entirety, is the Word of God written and is therefore inerrant in the autographs." (The society only belatedly added a second clause: espousing Trinitarianism.) Yet evangelicals have been in the vanguard of Bible translation around the world—a project that, ipso facto, puts rough-and-ready translations in the hands of inquirers and believers that in some cases only generally approximate the original Hebrew and Greek. Furthermore, those same inerrancy-defending American evangelicals (amplified by their British counterparts) have turned out such a torrent of translations, paraphrases, and study versions since the 1960s that the market is flooded with Bibles of various linguistic quality all aimed at helping the widest possible range of people accept, enjoy, and learn from the Bible.

The combination of populism and pragmatism goes a long way toward explaining why popular song is the art form most characteristically developed by evangelicals. Music is highly portable, both in the sense that traveling evangelists could transport musical instruments and singers more easily than, say, a large sculpture, let alone a cathedral, and in the sense that those who attended could easily learn the songs and pass them along to others. Popular song in its very nature appeals widely. It also can be experienced by many at the same time: thousands could hear a good singer or sing along with song leaders, while only a few could view even a very large painting. Popular music excites the emotions as well as the intellect. And popular song trades in vivid and intelligible lyrics that drive home gospel truths to people who might enjoy but would not fully understand a doctrine encoded in a splendid ballet or a sophisticated poem. (John Wesley referred to his brother Charles's hymnbook as "a little body of experimental [experiential] and practical divinity.")

Only by foregrounding populism and pragmatism, therefore, can much of evangelical behavior over the centuries and across the globe be understood. They both are in fact implications of the more traditionally recognized evangelical convictions regarding the Trinity, the Bible, conversion, and mission.

Conclusion

Our account of evangelicals and evangelicalism thus has concentrated where the scholarly consensus says we should concentrate: on the eighteenth-century revivals on both sides of the North Atlantic. We have met those Christians who recognized each other as spiritual kin and who then cooperated as they could. Their stories provide us a constellation of distinctive characteristics, an array that defines the nature of evangelicalism as a particular style of modern Protestant Christianity. And we can test the pertinence of our definition by simply looking to see if later evangelicals, like the ur-evangelicals, recognized each other as fellows and signed up to work together.

Over the history of evangelicalism, to be sure, certain evangelical leaders have found it expedient to define evangelicalism expansively so as to make evangelicals look as numerous and therefore as politically important as possible. Leaders seeking either protection from persecution or inclusion in power and privilege have drawn the circle as widely as they could. By thus claiming to represent, say, all conservative Christians as well, or all nominally evangelical (or born-again) people in societies historically marked by evangelicalism (such as the American Midwest and South), such leaders have baffled historians, social scientists, journalists, and other observers who have tried to get evangelicalism into sharp focus. Other leaders, to be sure, have been so concerned about preserving the purity and rectitude of their community against threats of spiritual and organizational declension that they have defined evangelicalism restrictively and thus excluded individuals and institutions whom those historians, social scientists, journalists, and other observers would otherwise have been sure would qualify as evangelicals.

The definition of evangelical offered here, therefore, is drawn from both evangelical profession and evangelical practice, especially in the original decades, the era of the ur-evangelicals. It ought to help both insiders and outsiders see that the evangelical *style* characterizes a great many varieties of Christians who have usually (if not always) recognized and cooperated with each other. Indeed, this book treats all such Christians as evangelicals whether or not they would and did use such a label to describe themselves. Christians who would not be characterized by this set of characteristics would thus not be evangelical and instead be either conservative or liberal, as the remaining stylistic alternatives.

The *boundaries* of evangelicalism remain both fuzzy and porous. So what is a pollster to make of someone who scores seven out of ten on a list of evangelical characteristics? It would have seemed preposterous to John Wesley for an evangelical to deny the Cross of Christ as essential to salvation, or the Bible as the sole authority for faith and practice, or the expectation of regular church attendance, while evangelicals have differed on even something as important in Christian liturgy as the Lord's Supper. (The Salvation Army, for instance, does not observe it.) Evangelicals are best discerned, therefore, as manifesting *all* of the defining emphases listed here in an integrated and reinforcing complex of concerns.

It would be wrong to look for evangelicals merely by setting an orthodoxy test, even as it would be wrong to reduce evangelicalism to mere piety or particular missionary activities. The whole thrust of original evangelicalism was toward the heart and the hands as *adding* to correct doctrine in the head. Even the great eminence of early evangelical theology, Jonathan Edwards, pointed to affections and behaviors when setting out marks of authentic conversion in his masterful and widely influential treatise concerning the *Religious Affections* (1746).

Evangelicals have seen themselves, therefore, as *generally* orthodox in doctrine, "orthoprax" in practice, and "orthopath" in sentiment. Moreover, they have believed that the Bible's own emphases have compelled them to put some matters above others. Unlike conservatives, evangelicals have not even attempted to hold onto every element of the Christian heritage with equal firmness. Instead, evangelicals have recognized each other as kin across denominational lines of disagreement. They have made concessions and bracketed out certain disputes to put first things first: the gospel of Jesus Christ, its proclamation, its fruitfulness in personal conversion, and its ramification in both individual and social transformation.

We return, therefore, to the constellation of emphases that distinguish *authentic, vital, and missional Protestantism*, what we are calling *evangelicalism*:

- Trinitarian
- biblicist
- conversionist
- missional
- populist
- pragmatic

Let us be clear that evangelicalism is not a matter of merely agreeing with such a checklist. It is a matter of living consistently in accordance with it. One might plausibly be referred to as a "lapsed Mennonite," at least in ethnic terms, or a "nonpracticing Anglican" as a person still belonging officially to, and retaining a vestigial sense of identity with, the state church of England. For the ur-evangelicals, however, the notion of a "nonobservant" or "nominal" evangelical would be a contradiction in terms—on a level with calling oneself a musician because one used to play the piano as a child or a football fan because one occasionally watches one's local team play. To find evangelicals worthy of the name, one has to probe for a combination of beliefs, convictions, and practices, since the whole thrust of evangelicalism is toward *lived* Christianity, not mere ideological correctness. Thus this book does not offer statistics as to how many evangelicals there are or have been in any particular locale or era, since authenticity and vitality are hard, if not impossible, to ascertain in large-scale surveys.

No element in this set of defining evangelical emphases, moreover, is itself unique to evangelicals—nor would evangelicals have intended any of them to be, since they typically have seen themselves as espousing merely "true Christianity." But however different evangelicals may appear and sound, however historically inflected their particular tradition might be—from Micronesian Free Methodists to Taiwanese Presbyterians to Kenyan Anglicans to Bolivian Pentecostals to Canadian Mennonites—if one comes across this *combination* of traits, one has met some evangelicals. It is commitment to Trinitarian theology and to the authority of the Bible in doctrine, piety, and practice that marks off evangelicals from liberals. And it is commitment to conversionism and mission, and the populism and pragmatism that those commitments entail, that marks off evangelicals from conservatives—whether Amish farmers, Anglican "prayer book" devotees, or rigorously traditional Lutherans.

Evangelicalism therefore is not merely a synonym for revivalism. Revivalism ipso facto entails a heating and cooling cycle, a flare-up of religious excitement that then becomes attenuated, dispersed, and domesticated—"routinized," in sociologist Max Weber's terminology—thus to become the "other" against which a new revival can arise. There is nothing in evangelicalism as defined here that requires such a dynamic. Each generation must be won afresh to the gospel and discipled in the evangelical style. Likewise, evangelicalism is not synonymous with evangelism, the proclamation of the gospel to those who have not yet heard it, or heard it properly. Again, each generation must be evangelized, but also sanctified into full spiritual maturity as part of God's global plan of redemption. The fundamental evangelical question is not whether one was once revived from stale, formalistic "social Christianity" or whether one was once converted from a completely non-Christian background, but whether one has been born again to a personally appropriated faith set on a course of lifelong piety and mission. As Billy Graham was fond of asking, "Are you a Christian *now*?"

Chapter 3
Evangelicalism expands

The nineteenth and twentieth centuries saw evangelicalism explode around the world. As the Anglosphere increased its influence, mostly via British colonialism and then through the global influence of the United States, evangelicalism spread to every continent and in many places caught fire. But evangelicalism was not merely an artifact of imperialism, whether "hard" or "soft," or of solely English-speaking initiative. From small missionary sparks many indigenous movements arose as well. By the early twenty-first century, evangelicalism was thriving in Africa, Latin America, and Asia—even as it was noticeably declining in the United States and fading away in "Greater Britain" and the European continent.

The passing of John Wesley in 1791 marks the end of the generation of evangelical pioneers. Indeed, it was more than symbolic. Wesley's influence over Methodism was so strong that only after he was gone did his successors in leadership feel free to do what Wesley had forbidden them to do: declare and construct Methodism as a denomination separate from the Church of England. Bishops Francis Asbury and Thomas Coke had become the leaders of a new American denomination in 1784 and Methodism would soon be recognized as a separate denomination in Britain as well.

Other denominations in America also metamorphosed to meet the growing challenge and opportunity of westward expansion. At Cane Ridge, Kentucky, in 1801, preachers set up a camp meeting to which people from the surrounding area could come for several days of preaching, soul-searching, and company with a goodly crowd of fellow believers happily housed in their wagons and tents. For frontier folk, whose lives were typically lonely and precarious, a few days in a safe place filled with like-minded people and offering spiritual excitement was a powerful draw. People soon traveled considerable distances to attend. Based on Presbyterian communion seasons inherited from Scotland, which annually extended over several days of preaching from makeshift platforms, praying in services and then extemporaneously around the site, and singing in anticipation of taking the Lord's Supper, these less formal "holy fairs" spread across denominational lines and up and down the leading edges of settlement. (The Hay Bay camp meeting of 1805 in Upper Canada drew 2,500 people, which was not especially large by American standards but constituted fully 5 percent of the population of the province.) In time, Baptists incorporated regular revival meetings into their version of the church year, and increasingly prosperous Methodists built cottages and even permanent homes on the most pleasant of campgrounds.

Foremost among the new revivalists was Charles Grandison Finney. Finney is sometimes given rather short shrift by scholars of evangelicalism. A budding lawyer who gravitated instead to leading revival meetings after a powerful conversion experience in 1821, his indifference to theology was such that when he was challenged on his knowledge of the Westminster Standards of doctrine as a Presbyterian clergyman—rather like a historian of the early American republic being quizzed about the Declaration of Independence—he cheerfully confessed that he had not read them. What Finney had studied, however, were the dynamics of revivals. He studied them, and he improved upon them. Finney employed a whole array, in fact, of "New Measures" meant to increase the impact of the revival experience. Among these were "protracted meetings," nightly meetings extending not just over the few days of a typical camp meeting, but also for weeks on end. Finney designated special seating in his auditoriums as the "anxious bench" for those in the throes of preconversion introspection (sometimes called the "mourners' bench," a device that would later morph into the "altar call" at the end of evangelistic services during which seekers were summoned forward for counseling). He introduced after-meetings in which such interested people would stay behind for more extended teaching and exhortation. And he promoted long public prayer services that sometimes included petitions on behalf of local notables, who were mentioned by name. Finney's novelties became standard operating procedure for many revivalists not only in America, but also in Britain, as Finney paid two visits to the British Isles and his *Lectures on Revival* (1835) became an international bestseller.

Finney became notorious for his guiding conviction that God intended revivals to succeed, and so God had shown Finney and others how to conduct them most efficiently. Finney was not claiming some sort of miraculous inspiration, but simply a pragmatic creativity that drew on both spiritual experience and common sense to construct optimal environments for conversion. Not to think and act in such terms would be as foolish as to buy a farm and then expect to harvest a crop by merely praying and hoping. His critics, largely from the Calvinist side, saw Finney as implicitly denigrating the sovereignty of God. God, they claimed, rained down spiritual blessing simply when and where God mysteriously decreed to do so. Not only was there nothing mere human beings could or should do to prompt this blessing, except to pray for it, but also it was positively presumptuous to do this or that with the expectation that God would comply. Finney shook off the criticism as misunderstanding. He had no intention of being presumptuous toward God, but merely of being obedient to God. God had showed him and others how to conduct fruitful revivals. These were the means of grace God evidently had ordained. Not to use them in faith that God would be true to his Word and produce changed lives, but instead to simply recycle the old and patently ineffective ways in hope that God might possibly deign to bless was irresponsible and disobedient.

This view helps explain what some observers have puzzled over as a paradox: a movement that promotes spirituality and prompts spontaneous and spectacular experiences being engineered by rational rules of public relations and organizational behavior. The likes of Charles Finney averred that to host such a revival is no more paradoxical than a pastor offering a congregation the Lord's Supper to provide spiritual nourishment or a physician offering a patient a medicine proven to cure a particular malady. Indeed, it was no more paradoxical than a manual guiding individuals to deeper mystical experience. Why not similar specificity of technique for communities also seeking more of God?

It was the entrepreneurial Finney who carried the bulk of evangelicalism with him: not only mass evangelists such as Americans D. L. Moody, R. A. Torrey, and Billy Graham, Indian V. S. Azariah, Argentinian Luis Palau, and German Reinhard Bonnke, but also the twentieth-century church growth movement, the booming megachurches, and other approaches to evangelism based on the social science of missiology. These innovations amounted to yet newer measures intended to practice principles God had shown had actually worked in producing conversions. Evangelicals would always characteristically pray for, rather than merely presume, God's blessing on their revivals. But they also typically invested considerable resources in infrastructure and advertising in the full expectation that God would bless what had worked before. This expectation became so strong that in subsequent generations good numbers of reported conversions were interpreted by evangelicals to indicate not just a gracious gust of divine wind but also effective work by the human facilitators, while disappointing numbers required convincing explanation to sponsors, not merely a shrug over the inscrutable workings of providence.

Revivals would continue to break out regionally over the nineteenth and twentieth centuries in Greater Britain and America—and well beyond. Wales, a hotbed of revivalism in the eighteenth century and beyond, was spiritually quiescent for the last half of the nineteenth century. But in 1904, Joseph Jenkins led revival meetings of increasing size and impact in a number of Welsh villages, and their influence led twenty-six-year-old Evan Roberts to see visions of what God would do through him as he took his place among the leaders of the revival. Whereas the eighteenth-century revivals in Wales had focused on impressive preachers such as Howell Harris and Daniel Rowland, this new form emphasized spiritual gifts and lively music in ways that mirrored the coincidental rise of Pentecostalism. This transdenominational Welsh revival lasted less than a year, but in that time 100,000 people were reported to have experienced conversion. The movement spread to Scotland and England, with estimates that up to a million people were converted in the British Isles.

The single most important revival in African history occurred among a transdenominational range of evangelicals in East Africa. September 1929 saw Dr. John Edward "Joe" Church, a medical missionary serving in Rwanda, at a very low ebb. He had left his native England two years before only to encounter a severe famine, his fiancée becoming ill back home, and failing his first language examination. He decided to take a break in Kampala, the capital city of neighboring Uganda.

One Sunday morning he walked up to the cathedral and encountered Simeon Nsibambi standing by his motorcycle. Nsibambi was a health officer for the Ugandan government. "There is something missing in me and the Ugandan church,"

Nsibambi said to his startled counterpart. "Can you tell me what it is?"

The two men spent two days studying the Bible and praying together. Both men were transformed, and Church went back to Rwanda a new person. The East African Revival had started, and it continued intensely for two decades, with effects lasting much longer. From Rwanda, it spread to Uganda, Burundi, Kenya, and Tanzania. In East Africa there had been much nominal Christianity under the imperial aegis, but low moral standards and a great deal of corruption even among church leaders. Moreover, the rise of African nationalism had strained relationships between foreign missionaries and Africans. The whole situation had been exacerbated by a split in the 1920s between two Anglican missionary societies. But the East African Revival brought healing and unity. Missionaries were humbled, stripped of racial pride, and able to enjoy deep Christian fellowship with African leaders, who also gained an understanding of Jesus's reconciling death so strong as to free them from resentment against the whites.

The revival brought to the fore native leaders, such as William Nagenda, Festo Kivengere (later an Anglican bishop and an associate of Billy Graham), and Yosiya Kinuka. Of the millions touched by the revival, some became twentieth-century martyrs in Kenya during the Mau Mau uprising, in Rwanda's tribal disturbances, and later still in Uganda as they opposed dictatorial regimes. (One of these, Yona Kanamuzeyi, is listed on the roll of modern martyrs in St. Paul's Cathedral, London.) Thousands of Africans were converted, nominal Christianity virtually evaporated in many areas, people openly repented their sins, and the church was thoroughly renewed.

Several decades later, revival arose in Ethiopia in the wake of the communist revolution's sweeping away of the privileges of the historic Orthodox church. The Ethiopian Evangelical Church

Mekane Yesus, of Lutheran heritage, exploded Pentecostal style from a few thousand in the 1960s to almost six million by 2020. (One might recall that Lutherans numbered among evangelicalism's Pietist roots. In the 1920s, American Lutheran Frank Buchman founded the Oxford Group Movement, a highly successful evangelistic enterprise targeting the upper-middle class through house parties that featured heartfelt testimonies of Christian experience. And Walter Maier's *The Lutheran Hour*, originating in the United States, became the most popular radio broadcast of its kind in the world, by the end of the 1940s reaching a potential global audience of almost half a billion.) An even larger African church was the Kale Heywet ("Word of Life") denomination that by 2020 numbered close to seven million members. Revival erupted also in Congo in the 1980s, and Congolese-founded churches became some of the largest congregations in London, Paris, and Brussels by the early twenty-first century.

Among the least-expected eruptions of revival in the twentieth century occurred in Indonesia, the world's most populous Muslim-majority country. Originating in the Indonesia Evangelists' Institute in East Java in the cultural upheaval following the failed communist coup of 1965, it was especially strong in Timor in the later 1960s, reporting more than 200,000 conversions. Although pastors and full-time evangelists were involved, this revival was largely led by laypeople, both men and women, some with scanty education beyond basic biblical literacy. Teams as small as three and as large as twenty would go out to villages on the impulse of what they took to be leadings of the Spirit heard through long and fervent prayer meetings. Healings as well as conversions were widely reported. Within six years or so, and particularly under the government's anticommunist insistence that every Indonesian must believe in God and choose a religion, more than two million converts were baptized on Java alone.

Scholars of revival pored over accounts of such revivals trying to find common elements that would explain them, while devotees of revivals studied them to find common elements that would promote them. But while the examples of George Whitefield and Charles Finney—dynamic preachers who gave careful thought to the techniques of revival, as well as to prayer and study—inspired most of the big-impact preachers in evangelical history, that history also shows that revival could come from almost anywhere and anyone.

Missions

Before Finney was sparring with his American Calvinist critics over the human role and responsibility in promoting revival, another pioneer was contending with his own Calvinist critics in England. Young William Carey, a Baptist cobbler who in the later eighteenth century moved over into full-time pastoral ministry in the English midlands, pondered the destiny of the millions of unevangelized people in Asia. Bringing his concerns to some local clergy in 1785, the story goes, he was roundly rebuked by a Calvinist elder: "Sit down, young man; when God wants to convert the heathen, He'll do it without your help and mine."

This answer might have been apocryphal. It certainly was, to be fair, Calvinistic to an extreme. Not only had earlier evangelicalism included Calvinists as prominent as Jonathan Edwards, George Whitefield, and Selina, Countess of Huntingdon, but also the Great Awakening in America was largely a Reformed affair. Indeed, Carey became inspired particularly by Edwards's account of the missionary career of his young friend David Brainerd among native people in the American Middle Colonies. Carey, himself a Calvinistic Baptist, persevered in his concerns and eventually wrote one of the most important tracts in missionary history, *An Enquiry into the Obligation of Christians to Use Means for the Conversion of the Heathen* (1792). Not content merely to raise the issue, Carey and like-minded colleagues formed what would soon be called the Baptist Missionary Society, and in 1793 he set off for India and one of the great careers in the history of missions.

Carey's story, in fact, became paradigmatic for many subsequent evangelicals, despite his record of failing to convert a single Indian through his preaching. "Expect great things from God; attempt great things for God" was Carey's motto. In Serampore, near Kolkata, he and his colleagues not only set up a mission from which they preached the gospel and planted churches, but also founded educational institutions (for poor children on up to seminary students), campaigned for social reform (especially against the horrific ritual of *sati*, the burning of widows), and translated the Bible into half a dozen major Indian languages. Not incidentally, he showed the missionaries' respect for the culture of their new home by also translating the great Hindu epic, the Ramayana, into English.

Translation was one of the great cultural gifts of Christians, and particularly of evangelicals, around the world. Over and over, preliterate societies had their languages reduced to writing and their grammars outlined systematically for the first time by missionaries eager to give them a Bible in their own tongue. Global literacy in very large part has been a result of evangelicals taking seriously this most fundamental element of culture and respecting their new friends enough to render God's Word—as well as many other volumes—into their own language. By the 2020s, the list of the countries with the largest Bible distribution included the United States, but also China, Brazil, South Korea, Malaysia, India, and Nigeria. More than 3,000 languages had at least some of the scriptures translated. An equal number of language groups still lacked a Bible but these were generally very small: totaling 250 million people. Still, over 400 translation projects were underway.

As many Westerners seem to forget, Christianity began in far west Asia, and the Mar Thoma churches on the west coast of India traced their heritage back to the Apostle Thomas himself. Christian communities came and went along trade routes, and in the early modern period the Jesuits in particular brought many tens of thousands into the Christian fold, most notably in the train of the inspiring sixteenth-century career of Francis Xavier, which reached as far as Japan.

Pietist and Moravian evangelicals were the true Protestant pioneers, decades before Carey set out. The Halle mission in Tranquebar, south India, became a model of missionary work: translation of the Bible; education of children, adults, and even clergy; a wealth of information sent home about those cultures; and a moderating influence on the colonial regime. The Moravians were the first to send laypeople along with clergy and were the first Protestant group to minister to slaves. Their missionaries reached the four corners of the earth, from Labrador to Alaska and from the Caribbean to the Far East. Where traditional denominations encountered resistance to minister to indigenous peoples, as was the case in Australia, they often turned to the German and Scandinavian Pietist and Moravian traditions for workers.

The Dutch and British trading companies, however, generally discouraged or at least tightly confined missionary work in their vast holdings—as such companies, as well as their imperial masters, usually did all around the world. Many colonial regimes found irritating missionaries' typical provision of education to Native peoples, which rendered the nationals more able to understand and negotiate with their European counterparts. And missionaries characteristically defended indigenous populations against both exploitation and eradication. So there was little evangelism of native peoples in the Protestant sphere of influence until well into the nineteenth century, as the stranglehold of those companies was ended by the more accommodating, if also deeply ambivalent, regime of the British Raj.

The denominational mission societies were pioneers, including Robert Morrison of the London Missionary Society, who arrived in China in 1807 and spent his days under a hostile regime quietly translating the Bible and producing a Chinese grammar and Chinese–English dictionary—invaluable to those who came later. But it was the coming of "faith missions" that boosted the missionary enterprise into high gear. The best known of these organizations was the China Inland Mission founded by Englishman Hudson Taylor in 1865. Unlike the denominational organizations whose well-trained staff tended to focus on colonial holdings along coastlines, Taylor recruited less educated men and, notably, women to bring the gospel to the neglected rural regions beyond.

The faith missions got their name from their practice (inspired by the example of George Müller in his congregation and orphanage in Bristol, England) of not engaging in formal fundraising. Nor did they incur debt. Instead, they relied on prayer—and, to be sure, a growing network of supportive correspondents to whom they, following Müller, rendered regular reports of challenges and successes. They also welcomed workers from across denominational lines, so long as they professed a common basic evangelical doctrine. The faith missions thus bypassed the typical constraints of distant denominational administrators raising (and controlling) funds and making policy on behalf of the missionaries. This new expression of populism meant instead that missionaries could do whatever God provided the means for them to do.

The China Inland Mission also took pages from missionary history (notably the career of Jesuit Matteo Ricci in the sixteenth century) to insist on identification with the Chinese by wearing Chinese dress and even the traditional queue (pigtail). They held worship services in Chinese houses and trained Chinese coworkers in what would become the "Three Self" principles of indigenization around the world: self-governing, self-supporting, and self-propagating. (Henry Venn of the Church Missionary Society in England and Rufus Anderson of the American Board of Commissioners for Foreign Missions—two of the largest missionary agencies—are generally credited with this formulation in the mid-nineteenth century.) Faith missions thus engaged vast new resources of personnel, prayer, and material provision for the missionary enterprise and became major players across the globe. China soon produced its own spiritual leaders who brought evangelicalism eventually to millions—notably missionary John Song, devotional writer and "Local Church" founder Ni Doushen (known as "Watchman Nee"), and "father of the house churches" Wang Ming Dao.

In Africa, missionary organizations spread south of the Sahara, inspired in part by the heroic story of explorer, missionary, and antislavery crusader David Livingstone of Scotland, who in the mid-nineteenth century opened up central Africa to the West—with the ambiguous result of both increased missionary work and increased colonization. Livingstone was typical of those who straightforwardly sought to bring commerce as well as Christianity and civilization to Africa in the hope that legitimate trade would quell the traffic in slaves. As is often true of bold and simple projects intended to right entrenched and complex wrongs, the results were highly mixed. Nonetheless, denominational missions from various European countries and North America were joined and even surpassed in some regions by faith missions, many of them inspired by the China Inland Mission—notably the Sudan Interior Mission and Africa Inland Mission. Such was the success of these organizations, amplified considerably by the work of Africans themselves, that within about a century, Africa south of the Sahara became a largely Christian continent. In fact, in 1900 Africa was home to about nine million Christians, but by the 2020s, there were half a billion, with estimates that this population would double to more than one billion in a generation. Africa made up 15 percent of the global population, but it held 20 percent of the world's Christians. Thus, while the nineteenth century was termed by Yale historian K. S. Latourette the "Great Century" of missions as Christianity spread across the globe, it was the twentieth in which the numbers really took off.

Several issues cropped up perennially throughout this narrative of evangelical expansion. Perhaps the most immediate and central was the often-controversial interaction of foreign missionaries and native traditions. While missionaries often defended the folkways, rights, and property of the peoples they served—much to the consternation of imperial and commercial authorities—they also sometimes advocated for governmental suppression of native customs the newcomers saw to be barbaric, even demonic. As the British Empire outlawed *sati* in India, half a world away it also abolished the painful sun dance on the North American plains as requiring what the missionaries saw to be self-mutilation to appease evil spirits. The British also banned the potlatch festivals among North American Pacific Coast dwellers as they had devolved in some places to a ruinous competition for status among chiefs at the cost of their impoverished tribespeople. The compulsory residential schooling of Aboriginal children in Canada, many of whom were taken far from their isolated homes to central institutions, became a vexed site of self-sacrificial missionary and educational service, heavy-handed and racist administration, and sometimes horrific and systemic child abuse. Meanwhile, African and Papuan evangelicals, both missionary and national, wrestled with deeply entrenched traditions of polygamy as highly problematic for the women and children involved while serving in many cases as one of the few options for unmarried women in situations bereft of legitimate employment opportunities.

Leadership itself was a perennial issue. Missions from more hierarchical churches, especially the Anglican and Lutheran, were much slower to recognize, educate, and empower national leadership and to countenance, let alone encourage, the more general reconstruction of Christianity according to the categories and customs of native traditions. "Lower church" missionaries, by contrast, typically put converts to work in every mode of service, not just as aides to the missionaries but also as missionaries themselves, and they saw the rise of indigenized Christianity in many forms.

Indigenous missionaries were often women, both because women often responded in greater proportions than men did and because patriarchal strictures in most, if not all, cultures meant that evangelism of women and children would proceed more effectively, perhaps only, from the mouths and lives of women. Thus Asia saw the training and commending of "Bible women" (India) or "virgins" (China) who both brought and taught the scriptures to women and children across what was mostly a vast rural landscape stretching from Persia to Japan.

Western missionaries were often female as well. Mary Slessor, a Scottish Presbyterian missionary, not only evangelized successfully in nineteenth-century Nigeria but also campaigned successfully for the rights of women and children. She stopped the common practice of killing infant twins (viewed as dangerous anomalies produced by demons) among the Okoyong. Indeed, she adopted every child she found abandoned so that some missionary compounds in her circuit became de facto orphanages. (It is bitterly ironic that some indigenous evangelicals in West Africa in the twenty-first century, in a fusion of Christian and folk beliefs, stigmatized some children as affected by witchcraft, a practice that spread through emigration to Great Britain.) Her story inspired several subsequent generations of missionary women throughout the Anglosphere. For decades, she was the single most popular biographical subject among student presenters at Prairie Bible Institute, the notable missionary training center in Alberta, Canada.

A second heroic woman also inspired evangelicals around the world and dramatically affected many in her home country of India. Pandita Ramabai Sarasvati was born as Rama Dongre in 1858 to a high-caste Hindu family. Her father, a Sanskrit scholar, broke with custom as he and his wife taught their daughter the language and, thus, many of the sacred Hindu texts. After she was orphaned by the Great Famine of 1876–78, she and her brother began to recite Sanskrit scriptures in public, and when she was

5. Indian scholar Pandita Ramabai Sarasvati was also an evangelist, social reformer, and founder of multiple charities.

twenty the University of Calcutta took the extraordinary step of awarding her the titles of Pandita (feminine of the word from which we get *pundit*—she was the first woman granted this honor) and Sarasvati (after the goddess of knowledge, music, art, speech, wisdom, and learning).

She continued as a maverick. She married out of caste and then, when her husband died after only two years, refused to sequester herself as a widow out of public sight. Instead, she took up the cause of educating all women and emancipating them particularly from child marriage. Her voice, and that of her Arya Women's Association, became so powerful it eventually influenced British policy on both issues.

In 1883, still in her mid-twenties, she traveled to Britain to pursue medical studies. Increasing deafness disqualified her, but while there she converted to Christianity. After touring the United States and Canada (she lectured also in Japan and Australia) and authoring a book promoting women's rights, she returned to India. In 1896, during a severe famine, Ramabai (the "bai" is an honorific for "elder sister") toured the villages of Maharashtra with a caravan of bullock carts and rescued thousands of outcast children, child widows, orphans, and other destitute women. She brought them to the shelter she founded in Bombay—later moved to Pune and then moved again outside the city after opposition arose because of conversions to Christianity. The resulting mission had a kindergarten for young children, a range of schools, a hospital, a refuge for "fallen women," cloth-weaving looms, printing presses, tailoring and handicrafts, a flour mill, an oil press, a laundry, a farm, orchards, and wells.

By 1900 there were upward of 1,500 residents in the Mukti mission. In addition to administration and teaching alongside her daughter, Manorama, as her trusted confidante and coleader, Ramabai managed to translate the Bible into her mother tongue—Marathi—from the original Hebrew and Greek. Indeed, she completed the revision of the final drafts only hours before she died in 1922, her worn-out daughter having passed away just months before. But the Mukti mission continued as a center of Pentecostal revival. Reviled by many in her lifetime as both a critic and an apostate of Hinduism, Ramabai was eventually honored in 1989 by a stamp issued by the government of India. The Pandita Ramabai Mukti Mission was active well into the twenty-first century, providing housing, education, and vocational training for widows, orphans, and the blind.

To be sure, women also came to the mission field as wives and mothers to exemplify and teach a more civilized way of making a home. Such a strategy was part of the "Christianize and civilize" dual mission of so many Europeans to Asians and Africans. Missionary women also helped to staff schools for girls that trained them not only in the faith and in homemaking, but also in skilled domestic service and even academic subjects—such that some traditionalists, both white and indigenous, became nervous about the elevated status of non-white women such treatment implied. Meanwhile, the inspiring accounts and testimonies of missionary women published in magazines and books back home helped to bolster the status of women in churches and families in the North Atlantic "sending" countries as well.

Evangelicals thus manifested a paradoxical understanding of gender roles in Christian endeavor. The sixteenth-century Protestant Reformation enhanced the status of women with the right hand but took away opportunities with the left. Even as the Reformers valorized family life as being no less spiritual than clerical celibacy, they also removed zones of service available to women in the holy orders of the Catholic church. Therein women could and did become scholars, writers, teachers, spiritual directors, and governors (as abbesses) of sometimes huge and influential organizations and estates. Little opportunity was left to them in the reorganization of church life propagated by the Protestants.

Evangelicalism, however, saw women resume positions of ecclesial leadership. Women were rarely allowed posts in theological seminaries, but evangelical populism promoted some women to become major speakers and writers. Phoebe Palmer, Hannah Whitall Smith, and Amy Carmichael were among evangelicalism's notable writers on, and thus teachers of, exemplary piety. Others raised influential voices on major social issues such as abolitionism, women's suffrage, temperance, and prison reform, including both white and Black leaders such as Hannah More, Sojourner Truth, Harriet Tubman, and Frances Willard in the United States, Canadian Nellie McClung, Elizabeth Fry in England, and the English mother–daughter team of Emmeline and Christabel Pankhurst. Women were sponsors and leaders of entire denominations, whether Selina, Countess of Huntingdon, and her Calvinist Methodists in the eighteenth century, Catherine Booth and the Salvation Army in the nineteenth, or Aimee Semple McPherson who founded the Foursquare Church in the twentieth. And women were the major supporters of foreign missions and served as missionaries themselves—ironically enough, especially in regions to which married men were afraid or otherwise unwilling to bring their wives. Indeed, it was the burgeoning of evangelical special-purpose or "parachurch" groups that most made available what the Reformation had taken away. Women became so active, in fact, that by the 1970s it became noticeably odd that evangelical women were welcome to do virtually anything but lead a typical white, middle-class congregation or family.

To be sure, given the global social pattern of patriarchy, the evangelical promotion of the status of women often disturbed the surrounding culture, as women were understood both as the spiritual equals of their male counterparts and as coworkers who were providing spiritual leadership alongside men. Evangelical teaching of male "headship" in home and church, if not also in society, thus served more to reinforce than to subvert the traditional subjugation of women, whether in Dallas, Texas, or in

Seoul, Korea. Indeed, historians of evangelicalism have noted a pattern. When revival fires burned hot, gender lines keeping women off the stage tended to disappear, only to reappear as soon as the once-radical movement began to seek respectability. Even so, evangelical teaching about the parity of women with men before God, the importance and dignity evangelicals typically afforded family life, and the many ways in which evangelical women exercised spiritual and secular gifts—from preaching to medicine to education to advocacy—often prompted persecution, if also occasional praise, from surrounding societies.

This tension pointed to the larger question of Christianity's relationship to the extant religions in a given location. The question showed up not only between Christians and devotees of other traditions, but also among the Christian communities themselves. Indigenization of the faith—articulating its doctrines, adapting its liturgies, and applying its ethics in ways authentic to each welcoming society—could sometimes become syncretism, the blending of Christianity with one or more other traditions to produce a new religion (with Haitian voudon, or "voodoo," perhaps the best-known example). Meanwhile, other converts were so deeply impressed by the fresh liberation they found in Christianity that they wanted nothing to do with their former lives and militantly opposed any combination of Christianity as received from the missionaries with their previous religions. Missionaries themselves ranged from outright rejection of everything native to a naively friendly willingness to compromise even basics of Christianity in favor of one or another tradition of a receiving culture.

Such tensions were usually more acute among converts in higher classes who had enjoyed a pleasing position in the old regime. Christianity tended to spread, however, not among high-status Hindus, Buddhists, Confucianists, or Shintoists, but among the poor, among minorities, and among tribal peoples (in both Asia and Africa) to whom both the gospel and modern European values promised a much better existence. It also tended to spread in situations of political controversy when Christianity could be linked to national identity—whether in tribal situations in Africa or in the case of the entire Korean nation as it freed itself from both Chinese and Japanese domination.

Evangelicalism, therefore, was already launched in many places around the world by the close of the nineteenth century, although it was only late in that century that the American giant—previously preoccupied with matters ranging from territorial expansion to the abolition of slavery to civil war—roused itself to the challenge of world missions. Largely a result of the influence of evangelist D. L. Moody and his student volunteer movement, the American evangelical foreign missionary force increased from 350 in 1890 to 4,000 in 1915. From there, Americans came to dominate missionary work for the rest of the century.

Indeed, the student volunteer movement, along with the Young Men's and Young Women's Christian Associations founded earlier (in 1844), gave rise to what in the later twentieth century became a welter of evangelical ministries to youth: Youth for Christ (which gave Billy Graham his start in the 1940s), Pioneer Girls & Boys, Christian Service Brigade, Campus Crusade for Christ (whose name was later shortened to the more culturally sensitive, if enigmatic, "Cru"), Youth with a Mission, and perhaps most importantly the International Fellowship of Evangelical Students—which by the 2020s had ministries in more than 170 countries. Evangelical success in resisting the general decline in religiosity in the West was largely a result of their ability to retain the allegiance of their young. These many groups, plus a lively tradition of congregational Sunday schools, youth groups, and summer camps, augmented by a network of evangelical schools and colleges and a growing array of sports-based ministries up to the collegiate level, did much to cultivate the evangelical tradition among those in their most impressionable years.

The turn of the twentieth century saw the large-scale New York (1900) and Edinburgh (1910) missionary conferences publicly aim to evangelize the rest of the world in a single generation. Such an ambition would have been ludicrous had evangelicalism not been successfully busy already for a century—alongside, to be sure, Roman Catholic missions particularly in French, Spanish, and Portuguese domains. The eruption of indigenous evangelicalism in those domains and others, however, came largely with the rise of a form of Protestantism that offered a distinct alternative to Catholicism and, in some ways, to mainstream evangelicalism: Pentecostalism.

Piety and Pentecostalism

While many evangelicals have focused on evangelism—getting the good news to people who lack it with the hope that they will accept it and be born again—many others, equally true to evangelicalism's basic principles, have focused on sanctification—getting those who are born again to grow up into spiritual maturity. The Oxford Club to which George Whitefield and the Wesleys belonged was called, after all, "the Holy Club," and holiness—complete dedication to God with the resulting goodness of life—continued to motivate evangelicals to seek full conversion, not just initiation.

The nineteenth century saw an intramural debate begin among evangelicals as to the trajectory of sanctification. Some, in congruity with the mainstream of the Reformed and Lutheran traditions, saw sanctification as a slow, undulating, upward curve of daily struggles with temptation, a kind of lifelong rehabilitation project of incremental progress. Others, however, did not deny the quotidian nature of spiritual training but also saw the Bible as promising what we might today call a kind of quantum leap, a fresh receiving of the Holy Spirit in a particular moment of intense cleansing and empowerment. Some, particularly associated with the annual meetings held at Keswick in the

English Lake District, taught a relatively mild version of this "second blessing." The believer should earnestly seek it, proponents said, but until it was received by God's sovereign grace when and where God willed to bestow it, one should just go about the normal Christian life. Keswick spirituality, also known as the "Higher Life" movement, spread throughout the English-speaking world as a spiritual renewal emphasis that bolstered piety without claiming the entire eradication of sin. As such, it made its way into Reformed circles as well as Methodist, Baptist, and other more revivalist traditions, with popular writers as diverse as American Hannah Whitall Smith (*The Christian's Secret of a Happy Life*, 1875) and South African Andrew Murray (*With Christ in the School of Prayer*, 1885). Even the twentieth-century preacher and latter-day Puritan Martyn Lloyd-Jones taught a "sealing of the Spirit" subsequent to conversion, tracing it back through Whitefield himself to some of his favorite Puritan writers.

Others, however, went further. Many bemoaned the way Methodism in both Britain and America was becoming established and respectable at the cost of damping down its original fervor. Under the inspiration particularly of nineteenth-century American preachers Phoebe Palmer and Charles Finney, some formed denominations intent on repristinating Wesley's doctrine that one could, and should, seek "entire sanctification," a "perfect love" of God here and now that would end one's appetite for sin and empower one to live a life pleasing to God except for occasional and unintentional missteps. These "Holiness" denominations would range from the small and sectarian—such as the Primitive Methodists—to the large and influential, whether the Church of the Nazarene, the Christian and Missionary Alliance, or the Salvation Army. Most would retain the plain, even rough-hewn, ways of typical evangelicalism. But there were a few exceptions, notably the Catholic Apostolic Church inspired by the Scotsman Edward Irving and led by Henry Drummond. This group championed healing and prophecy as well as so-called tongues-speaking (or the gift of the instant ability to speak in another language, whether earthly or heavenly). But they also engaged in a form of liturgical renewal, adopting such elaborate rituals and hierarchies they found in the Old Testament, the Orthodox tradition, and the medieval Roman Catholic Church. (This group thus inspired the high-church Oxford movement of nineteenth-century Anglicanism as well.) While the Catholic Apostolic Church itself faded with the decline of its "apostles," it had a profound effect on international divine healing circles and charismatic practice, the most eccentric and influential example of which was Scottish Australian John Alexander Dowie, whose ministry in the Chicago area (including the founding of Zion, Illinois) inspired many churches in South Africa. The later twentieth century also saw a couple of varieties of high-church evangelicals in America. Peter Gillquist, of Campus Crusade, led a small but highly vocal number of fellow staffers into Orthodoxy. Wheaton College professor Robert Webber more influentially campaigned to reconnect at least a minority of evangelicals to the glories of the early and medieval churches in a blend of evangelical, Catholic, and Pentecostal styles of worship, with most of his converts ending up in Anglican and Episcopalian congregations.

Most radical of all, however, were the groups eventually to be known as Pentecostal, a name derived from the initial descent of the Holy Spirit on the earliest Christian community in Jerusalem during the Jewish festival of Pentecost, shortly after the ascension to heaven of the resurrected Lord Jesus (Acts 2). In continuity with the Catholic Apostolic tradition, these groups taught that a dramatic experience of the Holy Spirit was to be expected some time after conversion. This "baptism of the Holy Spirit" (a term other Christians used for the moment of initial conversion) would greatly increase one's spiritual vitality and would manifest itself in spectacular spiritual gifts (*charismata*): prophetic words addressing individuals, churches, or whole cultures; healing of physical and mental ailments as a sign of both God's power and God's compassion; exorcism of evil spirits as part of a broader program of "spiritual warfare"; and speaking in other languages previously unknown to the subject—so-called glossolalia, or "speaking in tongues"—as a vehicle for praising God, delivering prophecies, and testifying to the presence of the supernatural. This promise of the Holy Spirit on an unprecedented level connected powerfully with the folkways of people all over the globe. Those who daily struggled with poverty, corruption, and powerlessness—all of which were exacerbated, Pentecostalism taught, by spiritual enemies—found herein a deeply resonant gospel.

Though scholars have traced harbingers of Pentecostalism back to the nineteenth century and to locales as distant from each other as China, Canada, and Australia, the most commonly told "origin story" of Pentecostalism occurs in the United States, and with brilliant timing: the first day of the new century. A little Bible school in Kansas under the leadership of Charles Parham held a service at the end of 1900 to welcome in not only the new year but also the new century. The service resumed on New Year's Day, 1901, and toward midnight, several young women began to speak in a language unfamiliar to themselves and everyone else at the meeting. The startled participants somehow concluded that the women were speaking Chinese and the phenomenon was interpreted as a new era for Christian missions. Now missionaries could forego the extended rigors of language training and immediately begin to speak the languages of their target audiences, just as on the original day of Pentecost in Acts 2. (Some missionaries, alas, really did set sail with this promise, only to find upon disembarking that what they were muttering was not, in fact, Chinese. The more dedicated remained nonetheless and enrolled in the language schools previously established by Presbyterians, Methodists, and others.)

A few years later, Pentecostalism emerged in a major American city and soon went worldwide. William Seymour, a Black preacher who had been trained in Texas by Charles Parham, had opened up

71

a small mission in a house on Azusa Street in Los Angeles. In 1906, revival broke out with manifestations of spiritual voltage that eventually attracted both crowds and the big-city press. Black and white people, rich and poor, educated and illiterate, male and female—all were encountering God as never before. And all, whatever else they were experiencing, were speaking in tongues. Thus Pentecostalism became branded, so to speak, as a second blessing manifest in glossolalia. (Only in the early twenty-first century did significant numbers of Pentecostal theologians query whether tongues-speaking was required for all who have an authentic experience of this sort.)

Pilgrims from other countries came to Azusa Street to catch the fire or, like Ellen and James Hebden from Toronto, to explore parallels to their own similar experiences. Individual congregations and whole denominations formed around this experience, among the most newsworthy being the ministry of Canadian Aimee Semple McPherson a decade later, also in Los Angeles. "Sister Aimee" was a proponent of the flamboyantly staged worship services that eventually characterized many successful Pentecostal congregations around the world, and she was one of the important pioneers of religious radio broadcasting in the early 1920s, another area evangelicals soon dominated. The International Church of the Foursquare Gospel denomination became her lasting legacy, taking its place among larger Pentecostal groups in the United States and beyond.

Pentecostalism also spread quickly into African American communities from the racially mixed congregation headed by Seymour on Azusa Street. The Church of God in Christ, originally a Wesleyan body, heard of the Los Angeles occurrences and sent its overseer, C. H. Mason, to investigate. He returned to its Memphis headquarters speaking in tongues. The church then reorganized as a Pentecostal denomination. By 2020, it was the second-largest Pentecostal body in America (only the largely white

Assemblies of God was bigger) and claimed almost nine million members in more than sixty countries around the world.

The early twentieth century in fact saw revivals erupt all over the world, most of them Pentecostal in style but not indebted to Azusa Street: Melbourne (1902), Wonsan, Korea (1903), Wales (1904), Mukti, India (1905), Pyongyang, Korea (1907), Manchuria, China (1908), the Heart of Africa Mission in the Belgian Congo (1914), Ivory Coast and Ghana (1914–15), Shandong, China (1927), and Rwanda (1936).

At mid-century, Pentecostal phenomena were spreading into mainline churches. American televangelist and university founder Oral Roberts became a Pentecostal preacher and faith healer in the 1940s and 1950s and for a while served in the United Methodist Church. His meetings, along with a few others', acted as bridges to older denominations. But it was the so-called charismatic movement of the next decade (from the New Testament word for spiritual gifts, *charismata*) that would see the fire erupt within Episcopalian/Anglican churches, Roman Catholic circles, Methodist and Presbyterian congregations, and other older traditions all over the world.

Although evangelicals in Latin America (notably Argentina), Africa (notably Ivory Coast and Nigeria), and Asia (notably Pakistan and Korea) could testify to similar outbreaks already, the beginning of the charismatic movement has conventionally been dated to Sunday, April 3, 1960, in, again, the United States. Expatriate Englishman Dennis J. Bennett, rector of the large St. Mark's Episcopal Church in Van Nuys, California, recounted to his 2,600-member parish his Pentecostal experience of being "baptized in the Holy Spirit." (Bennett was among a number of Episcopalians in that part of California who had experienced charismatic phenomena since two of their number had visited a Pentecostal church in the spring of 1959.) He referred to it again on the next two Sundays, including the Easter service, and on that last morning many of his congregation suddenly shared his experience. The resulting publicity, which included articles in the widely read *Newsweek* and *Time* magazines, pressed his superiors to ask for his resignation, and he continued his ministry in Seattle instead. The movement grew to embrace other mainline churches, in which clergy began receiving and publicly announcing their Pentecostal experiences. These clergy then held meetings for seekers and healing services that included praying over and anointing of the sick.

By the mid-1960s, the experience had spread to Roman Catholicism. In search of a richer spiritual experience and a renewed church, graduate student Ralph Kiefer and history professor William Storey of Duquesne University in Pittsburgh attended a meeting of the Cursillo movement in 1966. They were introduced to two books, *The Cross and the Switchblade* (written by Pentecostal pastor David Wilkerson along with writers John and Elizabeth Sherrill) and *They Speak with Other Tongues* (written by John Sherrill, who with his wife would go on to cowrite other evangelical bestsellers, such as *God's Smuggler*, about the daring missionary "Brother Andrew," and *The Hiding Place*, Corrie ten Boom's memoir of hiding Jews in wartime Amsterdam). Both of these highly influential books emphasized the Holy Spirit's gifts. In February 1967, Storey and Kiefer attended an Episcopalian prayer meeting and experienced the baptism of the Holy Spirit. The following week, Kiefer laid hands on other Duquesne professors, and they, too, had an experience with the Spirit. Students became connected with the movement through chapel services, and when Kiefer sent the news of this event to the University of Notre Dame, a similar event occurred there and the charismatic movement was fully launched. Indeed, it was this common experience of the Holy Spirit at the same time as divorce, abortion, and same-sex marriage emerged as cultural battlefronts that prompted alliances between many evangelicals and many Roman Catholics for the first time in their otherwise contentious history.

Similar stories were told across the Atlantic, and the Fountain Trust in Britain was founded in 1964 as a transdenominational fellowship of charismatics. The charismatic movement in the North Atlantic region burned brightest in the 1970s, subsiding in subsequent decades only to flare up occasionally—such as in the Toronto Blessing that attracted thousands of visitors in the mid-1990s to the Airport Vineyard Church to witness "holy laughter," "carpet time" (lying on the ground in spiritual bliss), and more. It continued to influence Christian churches globally—first through the Vineyard denomination in the United States and then through Australia's Hillsong Church, both of which became international factories of popular worship music. In no form, however, did the charismatic movement touch more evangelicals than in the Alpha course, an innovative dinner-and-discussion approach to evangelism and discipleship formulated in the charismatic Anglican church of Holy Trinity Brompton in London in 1977. In 2018, the Alpha website described the course as running in more than 100 countries and more than 100 languages, with more than twenty-four million people having taken the course.

Outside the Anglosphere, the fire burned even hotter and farther. One early site was South Africa, as the *Apostolic Faith Newspaper* written by Azusa Street pastor William Seymour began circulating in Cape Town. Azusa Street missionaries Thomas Hezmalhalch and John Lake carried Seymour's Pentecostal message personally to South Africa in 1908, and in 1913 Lake establish the Apostolic Faith Mission of South Africa. Also in 1908, Pieter Louis Le Roux, originally a missionary of the Dutch Reformed Church in South Africa and later a follower of John Alexander Dowie's unusual faith healing mission, joined Pentecostalism and established the Pentecostal Zionist movement in South Africa. By mid-century, the buttoned-down but effervescent South African David du Plessis had become the international statesman of the Pentecostal and charismatic communities to the World Council of Churches in the 1950s and the Second Vatican Council of the Roman Catholic Church in the 1960s.

In West Africa, as had also been the case in South America and New Zealand, Pentecostalism emerged among native traditions. In 1914, William Wadé Harris began his distinctive ministry in the Ivory Coast and then in Ghana. Clad in a white cassock and turban and holding a staff, Bible, and baptismal bowl, he confronted local spiritualities and shamans as the prophetic successor to Elijah. Villagers would bring their idols to him for burning and receive a tap of holy confirmation. Healings and other wonders, such as misfortunes to those who were not welcoming of Harris's efforts, attended his preaching. As rumors of Harris's powerful ministry spread, masses of people flocked to him. Hundreds of "Harris churches" resulted, while many of his converts also joined Catholic and Protestant churches.

At the same time, Pentecostalism was arriving in other West African countries from the United States and Britain, and within a generation so-called African indigenous churches (sometimes termed African-initiated churches) were booming as a result. At least in some places these churches were a direct effort to free churches from Western missionary control and cultural dominance, inspired as many were by the "Ethiopian churches" of the late nineteenth century that, across Africa, sought fully African expressions of Christianity. Happily, there were instances of a peaceful handover of responsibility from missionaries to national leaders. Indeed, the entire Sudan Interior Mission work in West Africa was amiably handed over to the Evangelical Church of West Africa (now known as the Evangelical Church Winning All) between 1954 and 1976. Sub-Saharan Africa thus saw the rise of a dizzying array of churches ranging from somewhat more enthusiastic versions of churches familiar to Westerners to fervent congregations whose doctrines and worship styles so connected with tribal traditions as to cause concern about syncretism even among some of their own members. By 2020, the church with the largest seating capacity in the world was not in Rome, Moscow, London, or Dallas, but in Lagos, Nigeria. Faith Tabernacle could seat upward of 50,000—more than twice the seating capacity of St. Peter's in Rome. And plans were being made in the 2020s to erect an auditorium to seat twice that number.

Pentecostal/charismatic Christianity exploded in Korea—such that the largest single congregation in the world was in Seoul. Founded in 1958, Yoido Full Gospel Church at one time approached a million members and, after commissioning many members to plant other churches and then enduring the shocking conviction of its founding pastor and his son for embezzlement, it still claimed a half a million members in 2020. Pentecostalism also became an important variety of Protestantism in China, a loose and in many places secret network of congregations that only sometimes conformed with government requirements for registration (as in the Three-Self Church). It blossomed into congregations both gigantic (as in hotspots such as Wenzhou) and tiny (as in thousands of house churches scattered across both the mushrooming cities and the remaining rural areas). Government estimates put the number of Christians in China at about fifty million by 2020, although many observers guessed that the true number was twice as many. As many as two-thirds of this number could be reliably estimated to be Christians of the evangelical style.

In Latin America, Pentecostalism broke out among a population long regarded, both by itself and by the rest of the world, as contentedly and continuously Catholic. Post–Vatican II priests attempted to formulate new forms of Catholicism to better respond to the needs of oppressed Latin Americans, particularly through politically oriented "liberation theology" and its revolutionary "base communities" of keen believers. The actual "preferred option of the poor," however, was Pentecostalism. This lively, experiential Christianity, with its unabashed supernaturalism, strict personal ethics, and strong family values, connected to the folkways of Latin Americans while it corrected the alcoholism and neglect of the family that was all too common. This reformation of manners as well as of spirituality brought new life to millions of Latin Americans, as it had renewed many similar households in Britain and North America in previous generations.

In the late 1900s and early 2000s, local and even national elections were influenced by evangelical voters and featured evangelical candidates. Indeed, by the turn of the millennium Brazil had become one of the largest "sending" missionary countries in the world. Fittingly, Saõ Paulo was home to a Pentecostal denominational headquarters patterned after the Temple of Solomon—except it was more than four times larger (roughly eighteen stories tall) and, quite intentionally, stood twice the size of the country's best-known Roman Catholic symbol, the statue of Christ the Redeemer overlooking Rio de Janeiro.

Many evangelicals were uneasy about, and even resistant toward, Pentecostals, even as Pentecostals often looked askance at what they judged to be mainstream evangelical declension into dull conventionality. Major evangelical fellowships sometimes took years, even decades, to admit Pentecostals into their ranks. Some evangelicals had relegated the "sign gifts" to the apostolic era, while others looked askance at the frequent appearance of a "prosperity gospel" that promised immediate health and wealth to all with sufficient faith (as manifest particularly in donations to the sponsoring ministry or church). Still others continued to prize an educated clergy steeped in the tradition over a charismatic one bubbling with innovation.

Nonetheless, Pentecostalism not only connected with evangelicalism around the world, but also increased its role in globalization. Globalization is typically discussed in terms of economics, politics, and popular culture: multinational corporations, regional or worldwide alliances, and the ubiquity of fads particularly in music, movies, and mores. But evangelicalism in the twentieth and twenty-first centuries became itself a globalized and globalizing phenomenon.

Evangelicalism's very nature, born out of its emphases on basic Christian doctrines, vital and individual experience of God, and a pragmatic concern for mission to everyone, meant that it could extend across all borders of the modern world and especially through the transnational migration of ardent evangelical laypeople. Missionaries themselves were vehicles of cross-cultural influence as they brought their own conceptions of civilization—often as an explicit part of the missionary package—as well as of the gospel. The agencies that sponsored them also sent fresh waves of influence to faraway lands, as when British missionary societies sought to dictate policies in Africa, Asia, and Oceania, half a globe away—policies that too often made more sense in London or Edinburgh than on the respective fields of missionary endeavor.

Evangelicals also sponsored cooperative fellowships of congregations, denominations, missionary societies, and special-purpose groups to advance its agenda of winning the world for Christ. Historians have noted a lineage stemming from the ecumenical cooperation at the Edinburgh Missionary Conference of 1910 and reaching to the founding of the ecumenical World Council of Churches in 1948. And when the latter organization seemed to swerve too far to the theological and political left in subsequent decades, the Evangelical Alliance—originally founded rather weakly in 1846—was revived as the World Evangelical Fellowship (1951), later the World Evangelical Alliance (2001), a group that in 2020 had members in 129 countries. Yet true to evangelicalism's populism and pragmatism, these fellowships of church leaders were largely eclipsed in influence by the globalizing special-purpose associations that connected so-called developing populations all over the world with modern techniques, technologies, and values—from World Vision to Tearfund to the

Salvation Army to the International Justice Mission to Bible societies in many lands.

Over the centuries, evangelicals had corresponded about and cooperated in various mass revivals, and the rapid development of transportation and communication technologies in the twentieth century dramatically increased evangelical news and collaboration. Evangelicals pioneered the religious use of radio: AM, FM, and shortwave—the last of which was particularly important in reaching into communist and other "closed" countries in the twentieth century. Superstation HCJB, "The Voice of the Andes" in Quito, Ecuador (founded 1931), pioneered long-range shortwave radio and by the 1970s could be heard literally around the world. The Far East Broadcasting Company (founded 1945) originally targeted China but expanded to cover most of Southeast Asia, as well as Russia, Ukraine, central Asia, and India, while its sister organization, originally the Far East Broadcasting Association and later known as Feba Radio, broadcast programs in Africa and the Middle East. Evangelicals became so prevalent on the later medium of television that "televangelist" became a word recognized in many standard dictionaries. Evangelicals made their own movies—most of them bad, but some with amazing reach. The *Jesus* film alone, produced by Campus Crusade for Christ in 1979, was seen by an estimated three billion people. And evangelicals completely dominated Christian popular music, such that the general term "contemporary Christian music" came to mean, essentially, evangelical pop. (Contemporary Christian music is not just a feature of the Anglosphere: "Tukutendereza Yesu [We praise you, Jesus]" has been a standard song in East African evangelicalism since the 1930s and a favorite since the 1970s in Kenya's booming Christian music industry.)

The career of Billy Graham nicely exemplifies many of these trends. He began as a small-scale revivalist preacher from the southeastern United States, but Graham's success in the media

6. American evangelist Billy Graham preached to more people than anyone in history. Here he speaks under the auspices of another major evangelical organization, the Inter-Varsity Christian Fellowship.

centers of Los Angeles (1949), London (1954), and New York (1957) launched him into the stratosphere of world celebrity, where he remained for half a century.

Graham was an entrepreneur of the first order. In 1947, he helped found a theological school, Fuller Theological Seminary in California, to educate people out of the fundamentalism in which he had been raised and into a broader engagement with culture. He also helped found the flagship magazine of the "new evangelicals," *Christianity Today* (1956), and his own ministry's journal, *Decision*, was for a time the most popular religious periodical in the world. Graham (and his staff) wrote a regular newspaper column that was syndicated widely (even appearing in, of all places, the *National Enquirer* scandal sheet); published a string of bestselling books; spoke on a regular radio broadcast; bought prime time on major networks for television specials; and presided over his own film studio (World Wide Pictures). His direct-mail operation in Minneapolis was so effective that executives from both major American political parties consulted with his staff. His mass meetings, the core of his ministry, set attendance records around the world, making him the preacher with the largest lifetime audience in Christian history.

Evangelicalism increasingly became a global culture. By the 2020s, the largest congregations in the world were not in Texas or Georgia or California, but in Korea, Nigeria, and Brazil. Christian worship music continued to flow not only out of Nashville and Los Angeles, but also out of Sydney and Nairobi, while the world's most popular church-based evangelistic program, the Alpha course, originated in London. Student leaders met each other at conferences of the International Fellowship of Evangelical Students across the globe, while affinity groups in many countries connected evangelical physicians, lawyers, scholars, businesspeople, and even motorcycle enthusiasts. Evangelical Bible colleges, universities, and seminaries—and not only in North America, Europe, and Australasia, but also increasingly in new centers of evangelical presence, whether Jos, Quezon City, or Buenos Aires—trained leaders from around the world for ministry around the world.

The Nigerian preacher Sunday Adelaja personified many of these developments. In 1986, under the aegis of a fading Soviet Union patronage program, he won a fellowship to study journalism at the Belarus State University in Minsk. Yet just before leaving home, he was converted by a televangelist and soon began an

7. **Christian contemporary music has many faces and voices, such as Canadian Steve Bell performing with the Winnipeg Symphony Orchestra.**

African Christian student fellowship in his adopted land. After the implosion of the Soviet Union, he moved to Kiev to begin a new job. There he and his wife began a Christian meeting in their apartment. Known as the Embassy of the Blessed Kingdom of God for All Nations, this early house fellowship of seven members ballooned over the next decade into a Pentecostal/charismatic congregation of more than 20,000, with rapidly forming extensions elsewhere in eastern Europe and beyond. He was criticized for preaching the popular "prosperity gospel"—the conviction that God wants to heal and bless everyone right now, not waiting for the world to come, so if you have enough faith, you will receive all you want and more. And he was accused, but not convicted, of fraud. Adelaja nonetheless led his church in undertaking extensive social work, later claiming to have rescued more than 5,000 drug addicts and alcoholics. The church also offered a wide range of Christian education and evangelistic media, from formal schooling to Internet resources.

Adelaja was no outlier. London's largest church, claiming upward of 10,000 attendees each Sunday, was Kingsway International Christian Centre, another "prosperity gospel" church, led by fellow Nigerian Matthew Ashimolowo. Indeed, there were many such works inspired particularly by Panya Dabo Baba, a pioneer of African missions to the rest of the world, among the most notable being the Redeemed Christian Church of God, a Lagos megachurch that by 2020 claimed to have birthed thousands of churches throughout Africa, Europe, the United States, and the Caribbean.

By the 2020s, roughly half the world's evangelicals were in Africa, a quarter were in Asia, and almost another quarter lived in the Americas—leaving relatively few in Europe and Oceania. Thus, even as Christianity in general was fading in Europe, in Greater Britain, and in North America, evangelicalism was burgeoning almost everywhere else—even in parts of the Islamic corridor stretching from Indonesia to Senegal. Indeed, mention of Islam and of the so-called prosperity gospel prompts us to consider the complementary story to that of evangelical expansion: the challenges, both old and new, that evangelicalism faced during those two centuries of astonishing growth.

Chapter 4
Modern challenges

As evangelicalism expanded, it did not always and everywhere thrive. Nor did it escape encounter with serious threats and rivals. Within Christian circles, in Western cultures at large, and in engagement with other societies around the world, evangelicalism faced indifference, resistance, persecution, and even the subversion of its most fundamental convictions. Clearly, however, evangelicalism generally flourished as modernity advanced. It is the distinctively modern form of standard Christianity.

The basic definition of "modern" is just "contemporary." Scholars typically date the modern period as coming after the Middle Ages, which means from about 1500 CE forward. In this elementary sense, evangelicalism is a modern phenomenon. But it is deeply modern in other respects as well.

"Modernity" is a word with rich and contested meanings. For our purposes, we will define it culturally. First, modern societies manifest increasing distinction and separation of social sectors and social roles. Education, healthcare, business, government, entertainment, family life, and so on each has its own distinctive values, sphere of operation, even diction. Second, modern people have confidence in their ability to comprehend the world with increasing accuracy, thus making continual progress in both understanding and controlling it (rather than relying on the lore of the past to guide our decisions, as is the custom in traditional cultures). Third, the modern world is truly a single world, an increasingly interlocking system of economies, political relationships, and cultural exchanges. And, fourth, modernity typically valorizes the individual person according to that person's particular qualities versus viewing people primarily according to group identities—whether family, occupation, clan, tribe, caste, religion, or nation. Modernity can thus be recognized where there is differentiation, confidence, globalization, and individualism. Moreover, huge advances in communication and transportation have connected far-flung societies and accelerated cultural change everywhere. It is within this matrix that evangelicalism has both manifested modern traits and contended with alternative expressions of modernity.

Evangelicalism has rapidly expanded in modernity precisely because its fundamental traits both reinforce and are reinforced by the fundamental traits of modernity. Furthermore, the distinctive variety of evangelicalism known as Pentecostal/charismatic Christianity has exploded in the majority world. It has offered a thoroughly modern religion while yet answering to the animistic spirituality of traditional faiths that have survived across the globe. Pentecostal/charismatic evangelicalism thus has not merely presented an alternative to folk religion (as other forms of Christianity have done), but has competed with folk religion in the same religious register. It has engaged unapologetically in prayerful warfare against evil spirits, cultivated spiritual immediacy in fellowship with the Holy Spirit, and promised this-worldly blessings as signs of divine favor—thus "fighting fire with fire."

Modernity has nonetheless exacted a toll on evangelicalism and may yet co-opt or conquer it. In fact, modernity poses several key challenges to evangelical religion.

Bible and doctrine

At the heart of evangelicalism—the primary source of its beliefs, the guiding written authority of its practices, the main food of its contemplation, and the chief symbol of its faithfulness—is the Bible. That evangelical heart beats in loyalty and love toward God, the triune God of Father, Son, and Holy Spirit. Modernity poses threats aimed squarely at that evangelical heart.

The most obvious of these challenges arose in fact as a pair: biblical criticism and liberal theology. These two modern ideas in tandem worked to remove the Bible and Trinitarian views of God from the center of Christian life.

The term "biblical criticism" does not imply a negative judgment, as in "He's so critical! Why can't he be nice?" The roots of the word are neutral. Criticism is like "sieving" to extract gold nuggets from creek-bed sand, edible grain from useless chaff.

Thus biblical criticism means just the scholarly study of the Bible, and in two respects. The first respect, which used to be called "lower" and is now called "textual" criticism, is the study of the manuscripts of a certain text, in all their variety, to determine as accurately and confidently as possible its authentic wording. Textual criticism of Shakespeare, therefore, aims to arrive at the definitive version of a particular poem or play. Textual criticism of the Bible aims at determining the most accurate text of the Book of Isaiah or the Gospel according to Matthew.

This form of biblical criticism has not posed much of a challenge to most educated evangelicals, and evangelical scholars participate in it with relish. Using thousands of manuscripts going back to the early centuries of Christianity, if not (yet) to the first century itself, scholars have pieced together Hebrew and Greek editions of the Bible that now approach the high-90 percentages in terms of scholarly confidence.

It was the higher, or "historical-critical," approach to the Bible that caused consternation. And even here, some clarification must be made. Any good student of the Bible asks basic historical-critical questions, since they aim to elucidate who wrote this part of the Bible, who the original audience was, what the occasion of the writing was, and how this portion of the Bible came to occupy its particular location in the canon of scripture. The aim is simply to get each part of the Bible into focus within its original context to help ascertain its meaning.

Evangelicals, therefore, practiced this form of historical criticism as well. What threatened orthodoxy, and thus evangelicalism, was a particular approach to historical study that came to dominate the scholarly community so as eventually to appropriate to itself the generic term *historical criticism*. This approach was critical in the negative sense because it undermined the authority of the Bible as traditionally understood. It discarded time-honored ascriptions of authorship: Moses could not have written the Torah, the crucial first five books of the Old Testament, and John and Paul did not write one or more of the various New Testament books attributed to them. Various prophetic books, notably the Book of Isaiah and the Book of Daniel, were considered a combination of at least two, if not three or more, documents by different authors, some of whom wrote well after the events they had traditionally been supposed to have prophesied. Indeed, if one looked carefully and knew what to look for, one could see that various books were themselves tissues of other previous writings and oral traditions.

Again, evangelicals had no basic problem with historical study of the Bible. Unlike Muslims, who view their scripture as the very speech of God recited to Muhammad verbatim and preserved miraculously word-for-word to this day, educated Christians understand the Bible to be composed by its human authors. Divine inspiration, according to careful renditions of the doctrine, means that God supervised the various elements of the composition of the Bible: from the events it depicts and the speeches it records, to the original accounts rendered of those events and speeches, to the minds of the authors who drew on those sources to write the various books of the Bible, to the editors who drew various collections of Bible books together, to the acknowledgment of the believing communities that these particular writings should be venerated as coming from God. Evangelicals took for granted that the Bible has its own history and that proper interpretation of it required an understanding both of how we got the Bible and what each component of the Bible would have meant in its setting within the canon. Indeed, what each scripture meant in its canonical form is what Christians have traditionally meant by the term *literal meaning*—not some silly, wooden refusal to see metaphors or parables as such, but as the common-sensical interpretation of texts within their milieux.

The problem facing evangelicals was not historical scholarship, but a scholarly tide of skepticism about authorship, about

8. Evangelicals are Bible people, and this young reader in Cameroon makes good use of his.

credibility (no Exodus from Egypt; no walls of Jericho falling down; no glorious monarchy of David and Solomon; no fulfilled prophecy; no miracles in the career of Jesus), and about meaning (the Torah is just a primitive Middle Eastern law code, and not a particularly impressive one; Jesus never implied, much less stated, that he was divine; Paul was a sexist not to be trusted on matters of church order). And, in an irony bitter to evangelicals, this skepticism was largely promoted by a movement intended to preserve the heart of Christianity in the face of modern intellectual challenges: liberal theology.

Liberal theology is commonly traced to the career of the German Reformed scholar F. D. E. Schleiermacher at the turn of the nineteenth century, although distinguished antecedents can be traced back through philosopher Immanuel Kant at least as far back as Luther's sometime antagonist Desiderius Erasmus, another scholarly clergyman. The word *liberal* comes from the Latin *liber*, for "free," and liberals are free to believe what they think is right without feeling obliged to submit to the authority of any tradition. Schleiermacher himself was raised in the home of a Pietist pastor and trained to become one himself. But when he encountered the dogmas of his Lutheran church as a student, he found many of them simply incredible. The Trinity in particular, he concluded, was not a mystery to be adored but a contradiction to be discarded. Thus, Schleiermacher wrote to his anguished father, he aimed to be a Pietist still, but "of a higher order"—one who lived by the increasing clarity of the Enlightenment to set aside conceptual mistakes of previous generations of Christians while retaining the true core of the faith: the veneration of God as modeled in the career of Jesus.

Liberal Christians sought to maintain the fervor of evangelicalism without the dogma, even as conservatives contended for the dogma while letting the fervor die out. Jesus was now a very good man who had a heightened "God-consciousness," the "first Christian" who showed us how to worship God, not to be the object of Christian worship. Salvation was no longer primarily a matter of receiving gratefully by faith the heroic act of God's self-giving in the suffering, death, and resurrection of Jesus through the life-renewing miracle of the Holy Spirit. As both Kant and Schleiermacher put it, the soul of Christianity was some combination of moral endeavor and mystical encounter. And the Bible was no longer a divinely given communication to be trusted and obeyed as God's Word. It was instead a record of the early believing community's reflections on its experience of Jesus Christ—with the Old Testament serving basically as "Jewish background" to the New Testament. (Schleiermacher at least once suggested the printing of Bibles with the New Testament up front and the Old Testament included, if at all, as a historical appendix.)

Liberal theology then departed more and more from orthodoxy. D. F. Strauss's reductionistic *Life of Jesus* (1835–36) was a mid-century sensation (amplified by George Eliot's popular English translation of 1846), and the end of the nineteenth century brought the definitive popular account from the great historian Adolf von Harnack, who summed up the essence of Christianity in a series of public lectures (*Das Wesen des Christentums*, 1900; published in English as *What Is Christianity?* in 1901) as "the fatherhood of God, the brotherhood of man, and the infinite value of the human soul."

Evangelicals were aghast. For mouthing such vague spiritual platitudes, Jesus was arrested, beaten, and crucified? Evangelicals saw liberal theology as stemming from a different epistemology and arriving at harmfully erroneous conclusions. Indeed, to evangelical eyes and ears, liberal theology was an essentially different religion, as Princeton scholar J. Gresham Machen put the point in his book *Christianity and Liberalism* (1923). Evangelicals increasingly ferreted out anything smacking of liberal theology in their institutions. And they drew up and enforced statements of faith that marked the nonnegotiable core of acceptable theological diversity. These were the new creeds of evangelicalism.

As for biblical criticism, however, the encounter was more complex. Evangelicals argued with the higher critics over their reconstruction of the history and nature of the Bible. But as the nineteenth century gave way to the twentieth, each side learned from the other. By the dawn of the twenty-first, many evangelical scholars operated happily under the assumption that at least some books of the Old Testament were composites, that some of the New Testament books attributed to Paul or John were composed instead by authors in their circles, and that certain prophetic utterances may well have been presented for literary effect as earlier than they actually were. At the same time, Mosaic roots of at least much of the Pentateuch were increasingly accepted by scholarly consensus, the dating of the composition of all four Gospels was pushed back to the first century, and those Gospel accounts were widely appreciated as simply shot through with the miraculous, whatever one made of such stories oneself.

The main bone of contention for scholarly evangelicals, at least, was the attitude with which one approached the academic study of the Bible. Late-nineteenth-century scholars such as James Orr of Scotland and B. B. Warfield of the United States spoke approvingly of "reverent" higher criticism—the study of the Bible that presumed (as Jesus presumed, they would typically say) that the Bible was divinely given and therefore was not riddled with ignorant errors or grotesque fabrications, let alone truly contradictory theological teachings. Rather than falling apart under hostile analysis into useless bits of ephemera, the Bible remained one book authorized by God and reliable in its coherent spiritual message. Irreverent Bible study, therefore, was both wrong-headed and mean-spirited.

Even more dangerous, again, was the liberal theology that disguised its deeply different dynamic and doctrine under traditional terms and thus deserved exposure as a false alternative religion, not merely another variety of Christianity. Denominational heresy trials thus arose in Germany, Britain, Australia, America, and Canada in the nineteenth and twentieth centuries.

Oddly, however, the most public trial involving evangelicals was not over the Bible or the Trinity, keystones of Christian conviction. It came in the 1920s and was fought over, of all things, paleontology.

Science and secularism

Despite the widespread belief that there is an inherent conflict between science and Christianity, such a conflict does not exist. The pioneers of the Scientific Revolution itself were, virtually to a man, believers in God, albeit believers of widely different views (from Catholic to Protestant to Unitarian). And scientists to this day have rejoiced in what they see to be the congruity between tenets of the Christian religion and principles of the scientific method—with Francis Collins, sometime head of the Human Genome Project and director of the National Institutes of Health in the United States, being perhaps the most prominent contemporary exemplar. As historian Owen Chadwick pointed out, however, when a high school student confidently tells his little brother that "Darwin has disproved the Bible," something has gone seriously wrong in the relationship of science and Christianity.

Evangelicals did not produce a unified and hostile response to the theory of evolution. Evangelical responses to evolution in the nineteenth century (and ever since) ranged from easy acceptance to outright rejection, with many evangelicals populating the intermediate points on the spectrum. Evangelicals could not agree with Darwin's agnosticism tending toward atheism, but the truly scientific question really had nothing to do with whether a

Supreme Being had guided the emergence of life on earth. It was whether evolution, and evolution largely via natural selection, was the best way to understand the origin of species. So-called creation science, arising particularly from the publication in 1961 of the popular book *The Genesis Flood* by Henry Morris and John Whitcomb, would declare itself the only true Christian viewpoint. It advocated a six-literal-day creation event happening in the relatively recent past with a subsequent global flood (think Noah and the ark) laying down sediments that fooled scientists into thinking that the earth is much older that it is. This dogma soon bedeviled schoolrooms, courtrooms, and legislatures— particularly, but not only, in the United States—regarding large questions of science, religion, and education. The more sophisticated intelligent design movement added fresh life to the cultural contest starting in the late 1980s as it argued for a mediating position between creation science and the evolutionary mainstream. It remained true, however, that evangelicals held views of the origins of the cosmos and of life on earth right across the board, as was evident in the diverse membership of the American Scientific Affiliation (founded in 1941) and then the later proevolution BioLogos Foundation (begun in 2007 by Francis Collins).

These sorts of scientific questions, however, did come bundled with philosophical questions about the nature of the universe and the existence of God. Darwin might have remained reticent, but several of his champions loudly proclaimed that his theory implied at the least no important role for God in creation, if not the very nonexistence of a deity. T. H. Huxley (who coined the term *agnosticism*), Herbert Spencer (the father of *social Darwinism*), and a score of lesser lights enlisted Darwinism in the much broader cultural struggle between traditional thinking, especially in Greater Britain and the United States, and new patterns of secular thought with roots in the more radical versions of the eighteenth-century Enlightenment. A static order created and governed by a paternalistic God had to give way, many said, to a dynamic world that was wide open to innovation—and on its own terms. Thus the philosophical outlook of secularism—the conviction that this present cosmos is all there is and that all truth and value are to be found within this world and not in either a world above or in a world to come—adopted Darwinism as its stalking horse in contending with Christianity. When communists gladly added Darwinism to their worldview, many evangelicals saw a phalanx of anti-Christian attitudes militating against Christian civilization itself.

Nowhere did this polarizing view of modern ideas as threats to Christian social order dominate more than in the United States. Evangelicalism—and particularly the grass-roots evangelicalism of Methodists and Baptists—had come to such cultural prominence in the United States that historians have referred to the nineteenth century as simply a "righteous empire" (coined first by Martin Marty). As late as 1900, a major missionary conference held in New York City would feature on its program of speakers a former US president (Benjamin Harrison), a sitting president (William McKinley), and a future president (Theodore Roosevelt, then governor of New York). Evangelicals were steadily losing cultural authority, however. (The decline was much slower in Canada, while evangelicals had never been dominant elsewhere in Greater Britain or in Europe.) Thus, particularly in the United States, evangelicals marshaled their resources to resist what they saw as a combination of liberal theology in their churches and the rising tide of outright secularism beyond—and nowhere more obviously and frighteningly than in once-Christian Russia, which by 1917 was in the throes of a communist revolution.

Higher criticism, liberal theology, evolution, and communism thus came together in the American evangelical mind and burst into public prominence in 1925, in Dayton, Tennessee. High school biology teacher John Scopes consented to let the American Civil Liberties Union use his teaching of evolution as a case to test antievolution legislation cropping up around the United States.

The trial was a public sensation, with three-time presidential candidate William Jennings Bryan volunteering to lead the prosecution and the greatest defense lawyer of the day, Clarence Darrow, representing Scopes. Bryan had the law on his side and won the immediate legal battle. But Darrow, Scopes, and the American Civil Liberties Union were on the side of America's cultural elites, and they won the public relations war. Fundamentalism was born in the popular mind—not as the urban, Northern, middle-class, and well-educated resistance to these various ideological and intellectual alternatives it had originally been, but as a rural, Southern, impoverished, and ignorant reaction against all things modern. And as fundamentalists lost the other major battles—for control of denominations, mission agencies, seminaries, and more—they retreated into a subculture of alternative institutions. Committed to preserving the fundamentals of the faith against contemporary compromise, they were separatist and militant, even if only selectively antimodern. (They would freely use modern technologies and sometimes insisted on ideas, such as creation science, that were not part of the central tradition of the church.)

These American evangelicals, in short, were afraid. They were worried about what was happening "out there" in the broader culture as liberal Christians were more and more evidently displacing them from cultural authority while outright anti-Christian forces threatened to destroy the American experiment entirely. They were also worried about what might happen "in here," and especially among their young people. They were so concerned about their youth losing their faith and being lost to "the world," in fact, that they formulated mores of a highly precise, vivid, and strict kind—and policed them rigorously. The old line "We don't dance, drink, smoke, or chew—and we don't go with the girls that do" epitomized fundamentalist boundary marking, and fundamentalists constructed a welter of alternative institutions—from schools to camps to colleges to magazines to radio programs—as safe alternative environments. This anxiety extended to doctrinal slippage, of course, and thus prompted fundamentalists to adopt their characteristic theological mode: defining doctrines extensively and insisting upon complete and unwavering agreement with them.

It is striking to compare the fears of this group of evangelicals and, say, evangelicals across the Atlantic in Africa, whose dominating concerns were poverty, colonial oppression, tribal feuding, disease, famine, polygamy, and spiritual warfare. For that matter, Black American evangelicals worried little about historical criticism, or evolution, or communism, or liberal theology while "Christian America" was still treating them so badly under the heel of the so-called Jim Crow racism that emerged after the Civil War. Even many white American evangelicals—notably in the Holiness churches (such as the Church of the Nazarene), Pentecostal/charismatic churches, Restorationist churches (such as the Churches of Christ), and Anabaptist churches (such as the Mennonites)—did not share the fundamentalists' anguish over the loss of a cultural authority they had neither experienced nor desired.

Much can be explained about the salient concerns of a particular group of evangelicals by determining what fears are being roused by a particular zeitgeist. Evangelicals can mount a campaign for correct doctrine in one community, a revival of warm-hearted piety in another, or a program of evangelism or social action in yet another, depending on what threats, needs, and opportunities they feel most keenly—even as genuine evangelicalism always maintains an integrity of head, heart, and hands. What seems obviously and hugely important to evangelicals in this or that situation will not even register on the consciousness of evangelicals contending with very different pressures elsewhere—which is why it is perilous to generalize about evangelicalism from the concerns of a particular evangelical community. (The twenty-first-century controversy over nationalism among white American evangelicals is a case in point, white American nationalism not being a major evangelical issue outside the United States. Indeed, nationalism waxes and wanes among evangelicals around the globe depending on how close evangelicals feel to the center of their respective culture.)

Evangelicals, in fact, have often so emphasized what worried them at the moment that they were all too willing to condemn fellow evangelicals who failed to share their fear and react in the correct way. The defining element was often a doctrinal matter, but it could be a question of spirituality, of ecclesiastical practice, or of ethics. This tendency to focus too much on particular issues of the day dovetailed menacingly with the general evangelical self-understanding that evangelical simply means "genuinely Christian." Evangelicals were thus constantly tempted to go far beyond merely disagreeing over this idea or that action to excommunicate each other as simply not evangelical, which was to say, not Christian. Despite all they would have had in common, which in calmer times would have been sufficient for mutual blessing and cooperation, the logic too often was this: "If you disagree with us on X, which (to us) is plainly an entailment of basic Christianity, then you must not be a Christian at all." So evangelicalism at various times and places devolved into fundamentalism—which, despite its name, typically does not emphasize only the fundamentals of the faith (as evangelicals typically do) but sees every matter to be a possible entry point of compromise and surrender to enemy forces.

It was the American fundamentalism of the 1920s, 1930s, and 1940s that was the foil for Billy Graham and the other "new evangelicals" who emerged during World War II and by the 1950s were influencing so much of global evangelicalism. Moreover, it is the deep roots of this particular form of fundamentalism in a vision of a (white) Christian America that helps to explain the startling re-engagement of fundamentalists with American culture under the leadership of Jerry Falwell and his Moral Majority in the late 1970s and 1980s, with Ronald Reagan—the former movie star, divorcé, and only occasional churchgoer—as their unlikely tribune. This heritage would help to explain certain key developments in American politics over subsequent decades, not least the unexpected political career of one Donald J. Trump.

Imperialism and social justice

Just to the north, Canadian evangelicals took a very different path. Evangelicalism dominated Protestant Canada—which was most of Canada outside Quebec—until the 1960s. Even quite liberal leaders of Canada's largest Protestant denomination, the United Church (which in 1925 drew together almost all Canadian Congregationalists, most Methodists, and two-thirds of the Presbyterians), typically phrased their agenda in evangelical terms at least until the 1960s. Meanwhile, Reformed communities in Canada, Scotland, the Netherlands and, indeed, America, contended with modernity in their own ways, whether by posing a robustly alternative tradition (as fostered by Dutch prime minister Abraham Kuyper and the Christian Reformed denomination in North America), by conceding much in terms of biblical criticism while retaining generally orthodox doctrine and piety (a stance typical of many British and North American Presbyterians following the Swiss theologian Karl Barth), or in dogged traditionalism.

Evangelicals in Canada and also in Australia largely got the social order they preferred, whether in terms of alcohol regulation, votes for women, Lord's Day observance, or increasing publicly funded welfare—which rapidly came to replace much of the former evangelical tradition of private charity. The Toronto *Globe and Mail* and the *Sydney Morning Herald* had been owned and operated by evangelicals (George Brown and John Fairfax, respectively) and retained much of the impress of their founders into the middle decades of the twentieth century. Indeed, it would take the cultural earthquake of the sixties to dislodge a fairly comfortable cultural consensus in Greater Britain, as it did elsewhere. Then, however, Canada, Australia, and New Zealand seemed to race each other, and perhaps also the Dutch, for the fastest secularization since the French Revolution.

In short, fundamentalism came to characterize much of American evangelicalism, especially among whites, even as it was much less important in other places. But evangelicalism (broadly speaking) became the main, if not the exclusive, form of Protestantism in many other countries of the world—from Latin America through Africa to East Asia—and these evangelicals remained largely uninfluenced by higher criticism and liberal theology. Thus when international church meetings discussed liberal trends in modern Christianity, some Western Christians found themselves perplexed by Christians in the rest of the world. Non-white, non-Western evangelicals did not generally resist the spread of women's ordination, since women played such a huge role in the leadership and constituencies of churches in many lands. But they generally dug in against the legitimation of homosexuality, a refusal that put white, Western liberals in a bind. Eager to recognize the scourge of colonialism and to cheer postcolonial indigenous movements, the liberals were flummoxed by the generally traditional ethics based on the forthright biblicism of their non-white brothers and sisters. Whether at the World Council of Churches or the global conferences of major denominations, long discussions often resulted in fruitless frustration. Neither side saw a way to accommodate the other's clearly different views and practices.

Ethnicity and ethnic difference, in fact, had played a major role in the growth of evangelicalism around the world. Missions usually succeeded within tribes and along lines of tribal alliances, only to be impeded by long-standing enmities. The same patterns obtained in terms of caste and other class distinctions: like attracted like. Evangelicals often made good progress along affinity networks, only to run into cultural walls of separation. And "native/settler" animosities constantly threatened the evangelical enterprise, with Australia and New Zealand offering strikingly different possibilities in such relationships among otherwise very similar societies.

Far more troubling, however, was the checkered history of evangelicals and slavery. It is true that parliamentarian William Wilberforce and his influential circle of evangelical social reformers, known as the Clapham Sect, spearheaded Britain's abolition of the slave trade (1807) and the eventual eradication of all slavery in British dominions (1833). A generation earlier, John Wesley had been a fierce opponent of slavery—"that execrable villainy which is the scandal of religion, of England, and of human nature"—and he encouraged Wilberforce to press on, with a letter in one of the last acts of his life, "till even American slavery (the vilest that ever saw the sun) shall vanish away." The American Methodist Conference of 1784 denounced slavery and gave slaveholders twelve months to emancipate their slaves. It was Moravians and Methodists who first brought the gospel to African slaves in the West Indies and the American colonies. It was from evangelical churches that rebellions broke out in the Caribbean (in Demerara and Jamaica), which led to the liberation of Britain's West Indian slaves in 1838. And Charles Finney himself inspired the founding of one of the first interracial colleges (and the first coeducational one) in the United States, Oberlin in Ohio. Alas, however, many evangelical preachers could be heard on both sides of the slavery debate. Whitefield and Edwards themselves had owned slaves, John Newton (author of "Amazing Grace") was converted while continuing to captain a slave ship, and racial prejudice continued to be not only condoned, but also perpetuated from American pulpits well into the twenty-first century.

Indeed, the history of Black American evangelicalism is complexly interwoven with this story, just as the history of minority evangelical groups is usually both associated with and distinct from majority history elsewhere. Black American Christianity was largely evangelical because of a tremendously effective "home mission" among African Americans—exemplified in the career of

Daniel Alexander Paine, a leading bishop and effective evangelist in the nineteenth-century African Methodist Episcopal Church—especially in the urban centers largely abandoned by white Christians. And as the religion largely of people who had suffered privation, scorn, and violence from others, including cobelievers of other ethnicities, evangelicalism in these circles brimmed with biblical themes of judgment, liberation, power reversal, and social redemption. Likewise, their churches served as crucial community centers as much as sanctuaries of worship. Some Black evangelicals in the United States, Canada, and Britain went so far in their practical response to racist realities, in fact, as to cooperate with influential whites to plant new free settlements in West Africa—Sierra Leone and Liberia—and in Haiti.

White American evangelical worries that liberal theology was reducing the faith to matters exclusively of this world scared that influential community away from its own heritage of social engagement. John Wesley himself had advocated for debtors and prisoners, visiting them often himself; founded schools from London to Bristol to Newcastle; encouraged the Sunday school movement (which was first promoted by Robert Raikes in Gloucester as basic literacy training for street urchins); edited and produced many volumes of inexpensive literature aimed at edifying and equipping the poor; and even regularly read and passed on medical advice at a time when physicians as a profession did at least as much harm as good and were often not available to the lower classes. (Wesley's medical record, alas, was no better than that of many physicians.) The ur-evangelicals aimed to alleviate all that was wrong with their neighbors' lives, not just to save their souls, and so did most evangelicals down through the subsequent centuries.

The nineteenth century saw the flowering of evangelical social reform: in abolitionism, yes, but also in women's suffrage; reduction of child labor and the industrial workday and workweek; public schooling for all; prison and asylum improvement; homes for unwed mothers; orphanages; and crusades against the blight of the working classes, cheap liquor. Anthony Ashley Cooper, the Seventh Earl of Shaftesbury in England, was chief among such campaigners and he died widely revered as the "Poor Man's Earl." The success of these ventures in linking legislation with evangelicalism's characteristic voluntaryism in charity as much as in piety—every bit as much as the ebb and flow of spiritually focused revivals—moved later historians to pronounce this era an evangelical century throughout the English-speaking world.

By the late nineteenth century, however, many evangelicals in the Anglosphere and in Europe were becoming alarmed not only by political socialism but also by what by the 1920s would be called the "social gospel." A notorious case in point was the suggested revision of Christian mission articulated in the "Laymen's Foreign Missionary Inquiry" of the 1928 Jerusalem missions conference and in the subsequent book *Rethinking Missions* (1932), in which W. E. Hocking and others seemed to ignore the classical truths of spiritual redemption to focus entirely on economic development and social reform. Evangelicals increasingly shunned the Student Christian Movement on Anglo-American university campuses in favor of the new Christian Unions (later the International Fellowship of Evangelical Students) out of similar concerns. By the middle of the twentieth century, therefore, anything to do with "social action" or "social justice" had gone into eclipse among many Anglo-American evangelicals as the domain of the liberals. Evangelical mission shrank largely to evangelism and the preservation of the civic freedom to evangelize. Even relief-and-development initiatives such as World Vision felt obliged to justify their work in terms of evangelism. "A hungry belly has no ears" for the gospel, they would say. So help us feed the poor in order that they may then be disposed to listen to evangelism.

It took young Latin American theologians—notably Ecuadorian René Padilla, Puerto Rican Orlando Costas, and Peruvian Samuel

Escobar—to remind the global evangelical community of what they called "integral mission." They spoke up insistently at the international conference of evangelicals held at Lausanne, Switzerland, in 1974 to remind British and North American evangelicals of the holistic gospel that evangelicalism had in fact historically preached and practiced. This was a gospel that emphasized personal sanctification as well as justification, plus social transformation as well as individual renewal. God cared about whole human beings, not just souls, and God intended to redeem the whole planet, not just people. Evangelicals typically had established missions not merely as preaching stations, but as centers of medical care, poor relief, education, political refuge, and more—from Sir Wilfred Grenfell's multipronged outreach to impoverished fisherfolk in the scattered outports of Newfoundland to the various agricultural and educational initiatives arising out of the pastoral ministry of Samuel Marsden and his successors among Maori and settlers alike in New Zealand and throughout the Pacific Islands.

The Latin Americans at Lausanne in 1974, like their counterparts in Africa, had never had to respond to a large-scale liberal Christianity that emphasized a social gospel. So they had never felt pressed to defend the one by diminishing the other in compensatory reaction. Instead, millions in the Global South gladly adopted the evangelical heritage of questioning established authorities, both ecclesiastical and political; the emphasis on individual literacy and spiritual gifting; the call to personal responsibility and competency; the insistence on holiness in every sphere of life; and the tradition of ministry of care for body as well as soul. The resulting Lausanne Covenant, drafted by the Scottish polymath J. D. Douglas and revised primarily by the English evangelical statesman John Stott—thus bearing their considerable authority in Anglophone evangelical circles—renewed global evangelical commitment to a hopeful holism in mission.

Not all evangelicals came on board with this larger agenda. Many continued to focus narrowly on personal piety. But many evangelical laypeople soon were supporting relief and development agencies such as World Vision, Compassion, and Food for the Hungry far more than they gave even to evangelistic enterprises. By the last quarter of the twentieth century, evangelicals had become conspicuous in electoral politics and in a range of broader cultural struggles stemming from the 1960s— from abortion and euthanasia to the liberalizing of divorce and same-sex marriage, and from sex trafficking to human rights violations around the globe. The most popular version of evangelicalism in the world was the Pentecostalism that assured believers of God's interest in their social and economic and political circumstances, not just their spiritual condition. Merely preaching the gospel to get souls into heaven was disappearing almost everywhere in evangelicalism.

Religious alternatives

The greatest challenges facing evangelicals outside the Anglosphere and the European continent were very different from those of the homelands of evangelicalism. In Latin America, evangelicals in several countries were now influencing elections in situations of almost constant social and economic upheaval, with governments from the left, center, and right coming and going sometimes at a wild pace. In Africa, especially in situations in which Muslim–Christian differences reinforced long-standing tribal grievances, warfare intensified along religious lines, sometimes amounting to attempted genocide. Even in nominally Christian areas, such deep-seated antipathies occasionally erupted into Christian-on-Christian violence.

Meanwhile, majority-world societies generally were characterized by terrible disparities of income, so that the prosperity gospel became popular, even standard, in evangelical preaching. Throughout evangelical history, whether among the British city slums served by the Salvation Army or the *favelas* of Latin America served by Pentecostal churches, evangelical conversion had brought important increases of personal dignity, reliability in work, temperance with alcohol, and fidelity to spouse and family. The prosperity gospel teaching went significantly further as it pressed believers into sacrificial tithing in hopes that God would be pleased and in return provide tangible blessings of health and wealth—a dynamic critics saw to be more typical of tribal religious transactions with beneficent spirits than of a biblical economy of prayer to a wise, sovereign God. (Such critics were perhaps unaware of how Anglo-American evangelicals throughout the nineteenth century and beyond had themselves typically seen success in business as a sign of God's favor.) Indeed, some observers wondered about possible syncretism in the popular "night vigils," attended by thousands in Korea and also across Africa, in which Christians demonstrated their conquest of the evil spirits that had oppressed them.

Nonetheless, many leading prosperity teachers also taught members to give generously to each other, not just to the leaders (that is, "to God"), and to generate jobs to help each believer find proper work. Many such churches held seminars to educate followers newly arrived from rural regions and struggling with the temptations of modern city life to resist debt and substance abuse and instead to practice thrift and sobriety. Thus the modern promise of material prosperity drew ambiguously on the twofold evangelical affirmation of both the goodness of this world and the priority of the next. And much evangelical preaching stood in tension with John Wesley's dictum, "Earn all you can, save all you can, and give all you can."

Evangelicals took different stances, therefore, toward their former religions, the religions of their ancestors, and the culture of the majority of people in their country. Some evangelicals starkly repudiated that heritage and adopted an only slightly indigenized form of Western Christianity, perhaps putting translated lyrics to Western tunes and otherwise worshipping mostly in ways inherited from the missionaries. The temples, shrines, mosques, or gurdwaras they used to frequent were castigated as strongholds of darkness, their former deities reviled as just so many demons, and anything smacking of the old ways shunned as backsliding compromise with evil.

Exorcism, in fact, played a major part in many of the triumphs of evangelical Christianity, especially in its Pentecostal/charismatic modes, across the majority world, just as acts of healing and words of prophecy also prosecuted spiritual warfare in a way that was most impressive to those from tribal backgrounds. These evangelicals developed a form of Christianity in creative interaction with their native cultures. Europeans had done the same already, of course, particularly in their festivals of Christmas and Easter that included and "repurposed" so many elements of erstwhile pagan lore. Even more relevant were medieval European episodes of outright "power evangelism," such as Boniface's public hewing down of the German Oak of Thor as a demonstration of the Christian God's superiority, which lay in the mists of Westerners' own heritage. First Nations in Canada and the United States led the way in such artistic recoveries and fresh articulations of the gospel in forms congruent with native cultural forms. The danger of syncretism always lurked at the door, of course, but the opposite danger of irrelevance seemed more worrisome to most.

By the dawn of the twenty-first century, therefore, evangelicalism globally understood was in a very new era. Evangelicalism had begun as a renewal movement in Christendom. It now was more typically a religion of recent converts, of people raised in quite different religious traditions who were catching up with 2,000 years of Christian history. They were coming to terms with what they should embrace, correct, or reject of their own cultures. And they were finding a path forward—religiously, yes, but also politically, economically, and socially—that would bless themselves, their families, and their communities both now and in the life to come. Thus the story of evangelicalism becomes much more interesting in our time, in terms of both its prospects and its hazards.

Chapter 5
The end of evangelicalism?

By the 2020s, many Americans had become disillusioned, even dismayed, over evangelical linkages to dubious politics. They pronounced themselves "exvangelicals" as pundits announced the death of evangelicalism. In the rest of the world, a range of challenges within and beyond the political sphere tested evangelicalism's integrity. Controversies over issues as basic as sex, the Bible, mission, and evangelicalism's very success posed threats that struck at the core of evangelical identity, purpose, and mission.

Basic convictions were not in serious jeopardy. Evangelical allegiance to Jesus and the Holy Spirit remained central. The main theological discussions among evangelicals were about second-order questions: whether hell will be eternal torment or a limited time of punishment terminated by extinction; whether hell is actually a form of purgatory leading eventually to universal salvation; whether the unevangelized yet have access to Christ's saving merit through whatever dim light of revelation they receive; whether Adam and Eve were literal direct creations of God or symbols of humankind's hominid ancestors; and whether women could properly be ordained to pastoral ministry as full equals with men.

Strangely, it was a conflict over what would previously have been universally viewed by evangelicals as a nonissue—right up until the late twentieth century—that took the greatest toll among evangelicals in Greater Britain and the United States while also challenging churches in Africa and beyond: same-sex marriage (SSM). Until the gay-rights movement, originating in the 1970s, evangelicals shared with the rest of Western culture the conviction that homosexuality was a disorder that at best needed to be curtailed and at worst needed to be criminally sanctioned. Over a single generation, however, the tide shifted in the modern West. Indeed, it shifted in two stages. The first was toward the legalization of SSM. Many evangelicals did not object to this process, whether because of a reluctance to any longer make a crime out of a consensual adult relationship or because SSM seemed a matter under the purview of the secular state for which many evangelicals felt no custodial responsibility. The second, however, was toward the full moral legitimation of all same-sex relationships, which was in flat contradiction to traditional Christian teaching. Thus evangelicals, along with many Roman Catholics, Orthodox Christians, and members of other world religions, felt put on the defensive as ostensible bigots.

By the turn of the twenty-first century, however, even some evangelical leaders were beginning to confess to changed views. Pastors first, and then a few theological scholars, went public with their stories of friends and relations who had come out of the closet and whom these evangelicals were loath to condemn as in any way deviant or deficient. So more and more evangelical churches, denominations, and other institutions faced dissent from within, as well as pressure from without, to expand their understanding of licit sexuality.

Evangelicals resisting the move toward greater inclusivity typically framed their answer in terms not only of the Bible's teaching but also of the Bible's authority. Proponents of SSM claimed to see parallels in scriptural treatments of slavery, patriarchy, and heteronormativity, with the implication that each of these was wrong. The people of God might once have condoned them, but surely not any more. Most evangelicals, however, took the line that these three issues were not in parallel. Unlike the ambivalencies and allowances in the Bible that pointed toward the emancipation of slaves and the full participation of women in society (even as some continued to qualify female leadership in home and church), the Bible spoke universally and unequivocally in favor of heterosexuality and against homosexuality. The debate, therefore, was not in fact about what the Bible says, because that was clear. The debate was instead about the authority of the Bible and its place in Christian ethics.

Evangelicals thus faced a fork in the road far more serious than the previous controversy about historical criticism. Many pundits observed a spreading refusal in the culture at large to submit one's reasoning to external authorities and to rely instead on the clear deliverances of one's intuition—or, as sociologists observed, the convictions of one's primary social silo. Many evangelicals were clearly bowled over by the compelling experience of one's beloved son or daughter, sister or brother, mother or father, friend or colleague testifying to their delighted freedom in owning their alternative sexual identity. It just seemed obviously right—so right, in fact, that unlike the extended and even exhausting debates about the ordination of women that had roiled Protestant denominations in the previous generation and that did result in a large number of changed minds on the basis of careful theology, surprisingly little actual theological work was undertaken to defend the legitimacy of sexual minorities. Loving inclusivity, so much a part of the progressive agenda of baby boomer culture, had become just evidently correct, and even evangelicals increasingly acceded to its persuasive power. The biblicism of evangelicalism was thus under pressure as perhaps never before in its history. Evangelical leaders in Africa, Asia, and Latin America observed with horror what to them seemed capitulation to liberal theological method by their counterparts in Britain, North

America, and beyond—while yet wondering how soon their own communities, bound in globalization to all others, would be facing their own disputes. (Indeed, in a drastic repudiation of this trend, a number of African states continued to criminalize homosexuality at the urging of evangelical pastors.)

This appeal to intuition in harmony with the zeitgeist dovetailed with the individualistic emphasis of modernity. Evangelicals right back to John Wesley and the Pietists who had so influenced him typically had established networks that placed believers within authoritative disciplines, informal social controls, and moral norms. Evangelicals had recognized the biblical teaching that Christian fellowship was necessary to promote sanctification, as well as to engage in mission to the world. Corporate identity and group solidarity were evident in earliest evangelicalism. Yet evangelicalism had begun, in part, as a critique of the existing churches as insufficiently pious. By holding their own distinctive gatherings, whether a Pietist *collegium pietatis* ("pious gathering"), a Wesleyan class meeting, or a Whitefieldian preaching service in a market or at a crossroads, evangelicals had put a question mark against the existing church bodies. At the heart of evangelicalism, therefore, has always been a critical tension between loyalty to what one views to be authentic Christianity and deference to one's congregation and one's denominational tradition.

Again, evangelicals have rarely been solitary in their spirituality. Evangelicals have not typically gone off into the wilderness by themselves to pray. The most radical evangelicals formed fellowships of like-minded believers. So to charge evangelicalism with sheer individualism, as many have done, or even to see it as a defining characteristic of evangelicals is not quite right. Evangelicals could be, and often were, schismatic—in the interest of preserving and advancing genuine Christianity, they would always say. But they usually quickly formed another, truer community.

Twenty-first-century modernity, however, saw many evangelicals around the world become progressively disembedded from thick structures of familial, tribal, and congregational loyalties under the atomizing pressures of both liberal democracy and consumerism. Their Christian relationships thus became noticeably more desultory. "Church shopping" became normal and, for many, interminable. Membership and participation in small groups meant to foster strong fellowship nonetheless came and went according to one's personal priorities for the coming season or even the competing demands of a particular evening. Charitable giving became a matter of personal attachment to this or that individual, organization, or cause, rather than a practice of tithing to a church and trusting its leaders to distribute the donations. Online "virtual" church attendance, exacerbated by the COVID-19 pandemic, became a new normal for many. Corporate solidarity, therefore, ebbed in the face of individual power to choose. And so did any sense of authority external to the sovereign self. The very voluntaryism that had unleashed so much evangelical initiative over the centuries had its shadow side. What was voluntarily undertaken could as easily be voluntarily dropped. And in a culture actively promoting a consumerist approach to everything, commitment was precarious, and the idea of deference seemed antiquated, if not actually antidemocratic. Individualism threatened the very evangelicalism that had in many ways fostered it in the modern world.

The lack of serious and sustained theological argument on behalf of SSM underscored the fact that evangelicalism as a populist movement had never engendered a serious community of intellectuals and artists who could read cultural currents and respond with a robust and constructive critique. Well-educated people were present at its birth, to be sure: George Whitefield and the Wesleys were trained at Oxford University, and Jonathan Edwards was a Yale graduate who would eventually be named president of the College of New Jersey, later known as Princeton University. Capable thinkers showed up throughout its history in key positions: Yale president Timothy Dwight led a revival on his campus in the early nineteenth century; his contemporary Charles Simeon was an inspiring preacher to generations of students from the pulpit of Holy Trinity, Cambridge; and Thomas Chalmers dominated Scottish ecclesiastical and, to a considerable extent, intellectual life in Scotland at the same time. A century later, London pastor John Stott, holder of a double First from Cambridge, would lead his generation of English evangelicals, and American historian Mark Noll, winner of a National Humanities Medal, wrote the landmark book *The Scandal of the Evangelical Mind* (1994) that pointed up the problem of anti-intellectualism he and his fellow evangelical thought leaders helped to remedy.

Nonetheless, evangelicals could mount only occasional and desultory projects to construct institutions to encourage first-rate cultural engagement. Even Fuller Theological Seminary, founded to be the evangelical counterpart to Princeton Theological Seminary, never raised the funds necessary to support faculty engagement in extensive, field-shaping research at that level. By the 2020s Fuller, like many other seminaries, was in financial distress. Arguably the most influential evangelical intellectual of the second half of the twentieth century was Francis Schaeffer, who sported neither an academic doctorate nor a university post. Schaeffer instead was a former fundamentalist Presbyterian pastor turned evangelist who popularized Christian philosophy for young people longing for more than the ABCs of the Jesus movement—the evangelical expression of hippie culture. His bestselling books encouraged a generation of evangelicals to engage in serious reflection and scholarship, but the scholars inspired by him quickly surpassed those books' superficiality as mere tracts for the times, largely forgotten a single generation later.

The situation was worse in other parts of the world, since the Americans had by far the most resources to work with, and first-rate academies cost a lot of money and take a long time to build. Acknowledging a growing number of exceptions from the majority world, by the 2020s evangelicals nonetheless could claim a solid showing in just a few domains: biblical studies (thanks partly to the Tyndale House at Cambridge and the associated Tyndale Fellowship), philosophy (with leadership mainly from the Reformed, Anglican, and Catholic traditions), and even the history of evangelicalism itself. Theology, apologetics, ethics, cultural history, literary criticism, art criticism, political theory, sociology, and many other disciplines crucial to cultural engagement continued to be pursued by evangelicals. But those who pursued them were mostly busy faculty members of small Christian colleges and seminaries, along with only a few evangelicals who had secured posts at larger universities scattered around the Anglosphere and beyond. The results were inevitably spotty.

The general cultural trend toward privileging an inner locus of authority also swept along evangelicals, therefore, even as it was recognized and bemoaned by evangelical intellectuals. It would have troubled John Wesley himself, who once confessed to a friend, "I am very rarely led by impressions [spiritual intuitions] but generally by reason and by Scripture. I *see* abundantly more than I *feel*." The great worry of the ur-evangelicals, in fact, was that their attempts to spark warm piety would detonate "enthusiasm," the wildfire of spiritual passion that led to the excesses of the Puritan Revolution of the previous century. John Wesley's much-admired colleague John Fletcher based his spiritual counsel on a careful combination of "the express declarations of the Scripture, the dictates of common sense [reason], the experience of regenerate souls, and the writings of a cloud of Protestant divines [tradition]."

In a movement dominated by preachers who often lacked even a basic seminary education, however, and who themselves appealed mainly to the feelings of the rank and file, an adequate response to this crisis of authority was neither forthcoming nor likely to emerge. For increasing numbers of evangelicals, the Bible itself became less a window onto a divinely ordained reality to which one had to submit than a mirror of one's own perceptions and preferences—confirmed by the like-minded people one could invariably find in the vast reaches of the Internet. The very valorization of individual spiritual experience that evangelicals had traditionally trusted to both partly constitute and partly validate their religion, without the equally traditional deference to the Bible, threatened to constitute that religion entirely—thus rendering evangelicals liberals in all but name.

Mission: conquest, cooperation, or an alternative?

Evangelicals continued busy in mission. But what model would guide their evangelism, church planting, and discipleship in this new era of global sending and receiving? By the 2020s, the pattern for missions had changed: no longer "from the West to the Rest" but "from everywhere to anywhere." The United States remained the largest exporter of cross-cultural Protestant missionaries (well over 60,000). But the second largest such missionary factory was India, with close to 50,000. Three of five of those missionaries worked in India itself, but in situations that were decidedly cross-cultural in geography, language, culture, and religion. Brazil sent the second-largest number of missionaries abroad, followed by France, Spain, Italy (each of which sent large numbers of Roman Catholics, of course), and South Korea, while the United Kingdom and Germany, heartlands of ur-evangelicalism, were no longer in the top list. The center of gravity of world Christianity had migrated over 2,000 years from Jerusalem to Timbuktu.

Mission had previously been conducted in one or more of five modes: conquest, counterpart, correction, completion, and cooperation. As evangelicalism emerged in Costa Rica, say, or Zambia, or Singapore, the question was whether it should simply supplant the alternative religions it encountered, whether by the

9. Missionaries go "from everywhere to anywhere." Sarah and René Breuel, originally from São Paulo and trained in Vancouver, baptize a believer outside Rome.

conquest of cultural imperialism or by the insistence on being an all-or-nothing counterpart, pulling people entirely away from their traditional communities. Missiologists suggested that Christianity grew best when the gospel instead came as a correction and completion to the extant religions, and especially tribal religions.

Evangelicals had always been pragmatic, determined to do whatever it took to get the gospel across. This could mean adaptation even of the logocentric nature of evangelical evangelism. Twentieth-century missionaries had twice visited a tribe in northern Nigeria known as the Gwandara-wara but both groups failed to have an impact. A third missionary group, which was composed of African members of the Evangelical Missionary Society (a fully indigenous Nigerian mission agency), learned that the tribe's name means "the people who prefer to dance." This name dated back to the tribe's rejection of Islam when it refused to give up their culture of music and dance for a religion that prohibited it. The evangelical missionaries adopted a new, and successful, strategy: they would dance the gospel to the "people who prefer to dance."

In Latin America, evangelicals had had to confront Roman Catholicism, indigenous traditions, and West African religions—as well as syncretisms of the three. At least as early as the Panama Congress of 1916, therefore, evangelicals had stressed Jesus Christ as the only object of faith and worship, the One who had made a full atonement for sin—thus obviating the need for any rituals even approximating further expiation of sin. No intermediaries were required between oneself and Christ, via the Holy Spirit, whether spirits of folk religion or saints of Roman Catholicism. Evangelicals in this locale brought a message and a piety of confrontational correction.

At the other end of the Americas, Canadian indigenous Christians constantly wrestled with the intersection of their ethnic heritage and their Christian commitment. By the 2020s, indigenous Christians were the most Christian of all ethnic groups in Canada, far exceeding the population at large, even those of British or French descent, in the proportion of their numbers professing allegiance to the faith. Most practiced an evangelical style of religion. Their regard for Aboriginal traditions, however—from smudging to drumming to dancing to the telling of tribal myths— varied from one extreme to the other. Some resolutely abandoned the whole package as paganism, while others fully embraced what they could recover or even compose of their folkways and made Christianity fit as it could. Most were somewhere in between, with tensions among believers often running high in local communities, congregations, clans, and families.

Adaptations to other cultural patterns, however, could be problematic. The major world religions—Hinduism, Buddhism, Sikhism, Confucianism, and especially Islam—proved obdurate to missionary overtures and often punished converts as apostates from the true religion. A clear break from the one to the other usually made the most sense. In Africa, therefore, evangelicalism often bore close resemblance to the spiritualism of native traditions—including themes of spiritual warfare, healing, and prosperity—as in Korea Christians prayed in patterns appropriated from their recent shamanistic past, such as their long early-morning prayer meetings. In India, however, Christians often stoutly repudiated their previous religion as positively demonic, while in Latin America antagonism could be fierce between Protestants and Catholics.

Missionaries, furthermore, could not help but be implicated in larger cultural issues of identity and nation-building. As it had been in Africa, the Americas, and most of Oceania, in China and Japan Christianity was linked to hostile European empires. In Korea, by contrast, Christianity had been useful in uniting the people against imperial Japan. In the late twentieth and early twenty-first centuries, moreover, Christianity faced emergent Asian states, particularly from former members of the Soviet Union, whose secularity offered no support and often dealt out persecution instead. In India the scene was different again. Christianity faced the opposition of a national movement toward *Hindutva* (India as officially Hindu) that pressed hard on alternative religions, and especially on Christianity and Islam as religions linked to previous foreign regimes. In many countries in Africa, however, Christianity helped weld together tribes otherwise deeply divided by long-standing rivalry and local religions.

As missionaries from many of these regions then reversed the missionary vector and sought to evangelize the post-Christian countries of Europe, Greater Britain, and the United States, therefore, they brought a wide range of modes of engagement to the task and experienced varying degrees of success. Since those countries were themselves home to increasing numbers of immigrants, however, as well as to populations themselves growing increasingly ambivalent about modern life, various modes could seem to be necessary in order to connect with various kinds of people. Thus burgeoning evangelical churches were not all of the same sort, missionally speaking. Some took a confrontational stance toward other religions. Others denounced Western consumerist affluence. Still others, however, preached a prosperity gospel that showed up among Australian and American evangelicals who were so happily comfortable with global celebrity culture as to be mocked even by the secular press for their "pastors with expensive sneakers."

Politics: engagement or entanglement?

By the 2020s, evangelicals were widely noted for supporting a populist president who opposed abortion and affirmative action while he advocated for the military and the market. This president was Jair Bolsonaro of Brazil, a country in which evangelicals played an increasingly large and public role in politics. Evangelicals were linked with right-wing politicians elsewhere as well. But the linkage has not been universal. Indeed, Nonconformists (that is, the non-Anglican Protestant denominations in Britain) were long aligned with the political Left, and Australia's left-wing parties have also enjoyed a measure of evangelical support. Canada's major left-wing political organization, the New Democratic Party—which had formed provincial governments from coast to coast if not yet federally— came to prominence under the leadership of a Baptist pastor, Tommy Douglas. And it was a radio preacher, Bill Aberhart, who founded another radical party, Social Credit, that formed governments for decades in western Canada. Perhaps most strangely, in 1980 the evangelical American president Jimmy Carter was defeated in his re-election bid by the new darling of many other evangelicals, Ronald Reagan. And evangelicals influenced and even personally contested regional and national elections in Brazil, Guatemala, and other Latin American countries, as well as across Africa from Nigeria down to Malawi and South Africa, on behalf of quite varied political parties.

Evangelicals have played prominent roles in governments as far-flung as South Korea, Kenya, and Australia, and their growing numbers across the globe meant that politicians of all stripes had to keep an eye on them. Under President Xi Jinping, in fact, the burgeoning evangelical movement in China was steadily more repressed, with public crosses and even whole church buildings demolished as part of the Communist Party's rising control of cultural life. Xi doubtless recognized that evangelicals typically have behaved themselves as productive and loyal citizens, but they also have a record of resisting institutional injustice, contending for religious freedom, and generally making things uncomfortable for regimes that demand total loyalty.

Persecution, therefore, was generally the lot of evangelicals in China, in India, in Muslim-majority countries generally, and in borderlands of Muslim–Christian encounter in Africa, especially along the beltway of the Sahel. Growth rates of Christianity in China were rivaled by those in Malaysia, Indonesia, and India—to the consternation of many in their Islamic or Hindu majorities. Perhaps not surprisingly, therefore, millions of evangelicals suffered the erosion or even crushing of their basic human rights under regimes insisting on ideological conformity—with the twentieth and twenty-first centuries witnessing the fiercest and widest pressure ever experienced by the evangelical tradition as it contended with the world's political varieties.

In many places, however, the issue of political engagement was open to a different question. When did political engagement become worldly entanglement—as Caesar typically demands all that is his and then at least most of what is left? Evangelicals have differed with each other on this question, with a wide spectrum of political engagement represented across the centuries and around the world—from Mennonite withdrawal to Methodist social

10. Members of Chinese house churches, unregistered with the government, pray, study, and worship with special intensity as they risk persecution.

crusades to postfundamentalist "religious rights" to a few state churches (whether Anglicans in the United Kingdom or Free Wesleyans in Tonga) to Reformed-led governments in the Netherlands and South Africa and evangelically linked presidents from East Africa to Central America.

Whether it was the lingering attitude of "white Australia," the revanchist crusade for white Christian nationalism in America, or milder versions of Christian chauvinism evident elsewhere, in the 2020s evangelicals confronted the challenge of experiencing diminished cultural power without resorting to reactionary forms of political resentment. Indeed, not only white evangelicals, but also evangelicals in Latin America, Africa, Korea, and elsewhere faced a peculiar temptation previously unknown in their history: getting some of what they wanted under the wings of dubious, if not obviously criminal, regimes—alliances that provoked resistance among their political opponents to anything religious that evangelicals might want to say. Would the evangelical desire for social reform thus impede the evangelical mission of spiritual conversion?

As Oscar Wilde (not normally associated with evangelicalism) once put it, there are two tragedies in life. One is not getting what one wants, and the other is getting it. When it came particularly to political influence, evangelicals across the Americas, Africa, and parts of both Asia and Oceania faced this challenge, even as many of their brothers and sisters elsewhere would have been glad just for a little lifting of political repression.

Success: boon or bane?

We thus have come a long way from those little German Pietist Bible study groups, the tiny "Holy Club" at Oxford, and the modest colonial congregations of New England. Evangelicalism has exploded around the world and in the world's most populous countries—even in such unpromising situations as China, Indonesia, Congo, and Brazil. Evangelicals now can affect regional and national elections around the globe. Their edifices command prime sites in many of the world's major cities. Their agencies are significant players in world relief and development. And while they do not yet have much impact on academia, mass media, art, and culture more broadly, the evangelical style has come to command the hearts and minds of hundreds of millions on every continent.

As persecution from deeply antagonistic forces continues to shadow the lives of many of those evangelicals, the survival of this generation and the faithful transmission of the gospel to the next remains of singular importance. Meanwhile, other evangelicals face the opposite questions posed by the enjoyment of considerable cultural influence and unprecedented material comfort. Will the gospel go deeply into the hearts of evangelicals softened by success? Or will it merely ornament an essentially unconverted outlook?

When tribal fury erupted in Rwanda in 1994, it left 800,000 corpses and millions of other people injured and grieving. Most of those people, victims and perpetrators, were professing Christians, and as many as half of them belonged to evangelical churches. Evangelical songs and sermons clearly did not indicate full conversion—not, at least, to a form of Christianity strong and wide and deep enough to prevent the ignition of age-old ethnic animosities. Evangelicals have often made things better in the societies they have served, but cultural influence flows both ways. The challenge for evangelicals in the twenty-first century remained the same as that which has faced every authentic Christian in every time and place: to seek first the Kingdom of God, and God's righteousness, rather than settling for, and even celebrating, a pale, narrow approximation...or an idolatrous substitute.

References

Chapter 1: Original evangelicalism

David Garrick, "I would give a hundred guineas if I could say 'O!' like Mr. Whitefield": quoted in Edward S. Ninde, *George Whitefield: Prophet—Preacher* (New York: Abingdon, 1924), 162.

John Wesley's "Aldersgate experience": John Wesley and Charles Wesley, *John and Charles Wesley: Selected Prayers, Hymns, Journal Notes, Sermons, Letters and Treatises*, ed. Albert C. Outler (New York: Paulist Press, 1981), 107.

Chapter 2: Evangelicalism defined

Charles Wesley, "Father of Everlasting Grace," in John Wesley and Charles Wesley, *John and Charles Wesley: Selected Prayers, Hymns, Journal Notes, Sermons, Letters and Treatises*, ed. Albert C. Outler (New York: Paulist Press, 1981), 226–227.

"Pervasive interpretive pluralism," Christian Smith, *The Bible Made Impossible: Why Biblicism Is Not a Truly Evangelical Reading of Scripture* (Grand Rapids, MI: Brazos, 2011).

Charles Wesley, "With us no melancholy void," in John Wesley and Charles Wesley, *John and Charles Wesley: Selected Prayers, Hymns, Journal Notes, Sermons, Letters and Treatises*, ed. Albert C. Outler (New York: Paulist Press, 1981), 205.

John Wesley, "Lose no opportunity of doing good," in John Wesley and Charles Wesley, *John and Charles Wesley: Selected Prayers, Hymns, Journal Notes, Sermons, Letters and Treatises*, ed. Albert C. Outler (New York: Paulist Press, 1981), 364.

George Whitefield, "I saw regenerate souls . . .": George Whitefield, *Journals* (London: Banner of Truth, 1960), 458.

Evangelical Alliance 1846 statement of faith, Philip Schaff and David S. Schaff, eds. *The Creeds of Christendom*, 6th ed., 3 vols. (Grand Rapids, MI: Baker, 1931), 827–828.

John Wesley, "We have out of necessity varied [from the Church of England] in some points of discipline," in John Wesley and Charles Wesley, *John and Charles Wesley: Selected Prayers, Hymns, Journal Notes, Sermons, Letters and Treatises*, ed. Albert C. Outler (New York: Paulist Press, 1981), 54–55.

John Wesley re. Charles Wesley's hymnbook as "a little body of experimental and practical divinity," in John Wesley and Charles Wesley, *John and Charles Wesley: Selected Prayers, Hymns, Journal Notes, Sermons, Letters and Treatises*, ed. Albert C. Outler (New York: Paulist Press, 1981), 176.

Chapter 3: Evangelicalism expands

Statistics on African Christianity in 2020—and on the rest of the world as well—are available from the Center for Global Christianity at Gordon-Conwell Theological Seminary, Wenham, MA, and the Pew Research Center, Washington, DC.

"The American evangelical foreign missionary force increased from 350 in 1890 to 4,000 in 1915": Timothy Yates, *Christian Mission in the Twentieth Century* (Cambridge: Cambridge University Press, 1994), 14.

Chapter 4: Modern challenges

"Fighting fire with fire": David Martin, "Evangelical Expansion in Global Society," in *Christianity Reborn: The Global Expansion of Evangelicalism in the Twentieth Century*, ed. Donald M. Lewis (Grand Rapids, MI: Eerdmans, 2004), 283.

"The fatherhood of God": Adolf von Harnack, *What Is Christianity?*, trans. Thomas Bailey Saunders (Gloucester, MA: Peter Smith, 1978).

"Darwin has disproved the Bible": Owen Chadwick, *The Victorian Church*, 3rd ed., 2 vols. (London: Adam and Charles Black, 1971), 1:164.

Martin E. Marty, *Righteous Empire: The Protestant Experience in America* (New York: Harper & Row, 1970).

John Wesley on slavery, in John Wesley and Charles Wesley, *John and Charles Wesley: Selected Prayers, Hymns, Journal Notes, Sermons, Letters and Treatises*, ed. Albert C. Outler (New York: Paulist Press, 1981), 170–171.

Chapter 5: The end of evangelicalism?

John Wesley, "I am very rarely led by impressions," in John Wesley and Charles Wesley, *John and Charles Wesley: Selected Prayers, Hymns, Journal Notes, Sermons, Letters and Treatises*, ed. Albert C. Outler (New York: Paulist Press, 1981), xiii.

John Fletcher, "the express declarations of the Scripture": John Fletcher, *Five Checks to Antinomianism*, vol. 1 of *The Works of John Fletcher*, ed. Jeffrey Wallace (Brookfield, MO: Apprehending Truth, 2011 [1771]), 134.

"from Jerusalem to Timbuktu": Brian C. Stiller, *From Jerusalem to Timbuktu: A World Tour of the Spread of Christianity* (Downers Grove, IL: InterVarsity Press, 2018).

John Wesley and Charles Wesley, *John and Charles Wesley: Selected Prayers, Hymns, Journal Notes, Sermons, Letters and Treatises*, ed. Albert C. Outler (New York: Paulist Press, 1981).

Further reading

Atherstone, Andrew, and David Ceri Jones, eds. *The Routledge Research Companion of the History of Evangelicalism*. New York: Routledge, 2019.

Bebbington, David W. *Evangelicalism in Modern Britain: A History from the 1730s to the 1980s*. London: Unwin Hyman, 1989.

Bebbington, David W. *The Evangelical Quadrilateral: Characterizing the British Gospel Movement*. Waco, TX: Baylor University Press, 2021.

Bebbington, David, and Mark A. Noll, gen. eds. *History of Evangelicalism Series: People, Movements and Ideas in the English-Speaking World*. 5 vols. Leicester, UK: IVP, 2004–17.

Coleman, Simon, and Rosalind I. J. Hackett, eds. *The Anthropology of Global Pentecostalism and Evangelicalism*. New York: New York University Press, 2015.

Hindmarsh, Bruce. *The Spirit of Early Evangelicalism: True Religion in a Modern World*. New York: Oxford University Press, 2018.

Hutchinson, Mark, and John Wolffe. *A Short History of Global Evangelicalism*. New York: Cambridge University Press, 2012.

Jenkins, Philip. *The Next Christendom: The Coming of Global Christianity*. 3rd ed. Oxford: Oxford University Press, 2011.

Larsen, Timothy, ed. *Biographical Dictionary of Evangelicals*. Downers Grove, IL: InterVarsity Press, 2003.

Larsen, Timothy, and Daniel J. Treier, eds. *The Cambridge Companion to Evangelical Theology*. Cambridge: Cambridge University Press, 2007.

Lewis, Donald M., ed. *The Blackwell Dictionary of Evangelical Biography*. 2 vols. Oxford: Basil Blackwell, 1995.

Lewis, Donald M., and Richard V. Pierard, eds. *Global Evangelicalism: Theology, History and Culture in Regional Perspective*. Downers Grove, IL: InterVarsity Press, 2014.

Marsden, George M. *Fundamentalism and American Culture: The Shaping of Twentieth-Century Evangelicalism 1870–1925*. New York: Oxford University Press, 1980.

Martin, David. *Pentecostalism: The World Their Parish*. Oxford: Blackwell, 2002.

McDermott, Gerald R., ed. *The Oxford Handbook of Evangelical Theology*. Oxford: Oxford University Press, 2013.

Noll, Mark A. *The Scandal of the Evangelical Mind*. Grand Rapids, MI: Eerdmans, 1994.

Noll, Mark A., David W. Bebbington, and George M. Marsden, eds. *Evangelicals: Who They Have Been, Are Now, and Could Be*. Grand Rapids, MI: Eerdmans, 2019.

Robert, Dana L. *Christian Mission: How Christianity Became a World Religion*. Hoboken, NJ: Wiley–Blackwell, 2009.

Sanneh, Lamin. *Translating the Message: The Missionary Impact on Culture*. 2nd ed. Maryknoll, NY: Orbis, 2009.

Stanley, Brian. *Christianity in the Twentieth Century: A World History*. Princeton, NJ: Princeton University Press, 2018.

Stanley, Brian, ed. *Missions, Nationalism, and the End of Empire*. Grand Rapids, MI: Eerdmans, 2004.

Stiller, Brian C., Todd M. Johnson, Karen Stiller, and Mark Hutchinson, eds. *Evangelicals around the World: A Global Handbook for the 21st Century*. Nashville, TN: Thomas Nelson, 2015.

Walls, Andrew. *The Missionary Movement in Christian History: Studies in the Transmission of Faith*. Maryknoll, NY: Orbis, 1996.

Ward, W. R. *The Protestant Evangelical Awakening*. Cambridge: Cambridge University Press, 1992.

Index

Index

Evangelicalism